Poetry in Motion

Cheshire Vol I

Edited by Annabel Cook

First published in Great Britain in 2004 by:
Young Writers
Remus House
Coltsfoot Drive
Peterborough
PE2 9JX
Telephone: 01733 890066
Website: www.youngwriters.co.uk

SB ISBN 1 84460 329 6

Foreword

This year, the Young Writers' 'Poetry In Motion' competition proudly presents a showcase of the best poetic talent selected from over 40,000 up-and-coming writers nationwide.

Young Writers was established in 1991 to promote the reading and writing of poetry within schools and to the youth of today. Our books nurture and inspire confidence in the ability of young writers and provide a snapshot of poems written in schools and at home by budding poets of the future.

The thought effort, imagination and hard work put into each poem impressed us all and the task of selecting poems was a difficult but nevertheless enjoyable experience.

We hope you are as pleased as we are with the final selection and that you and your family continue to be entertained with *Poetry In Motion Cheshire Vol I* for many years to come.

CONTENTS

Ben Smith (11)   55
Annabel Tomlinson (11)   56
Nicholas Hampson (11)   57
Simon Roberts (11)   58
James Dickens (12)   59
Alex Gaut (11)   60
Jacob Murphy (11)   61
Sophie Large (11)   61
Katey Sadler (11)   62

Chesnut Lodge School
Sean Campbell (11)   63
Nathan McKie (14)   64
Daniel Reed (13)   65
Natalie Lindsay (12)   66
Joshua Astill (12)   66
Jane Parker (13)   67
Chelsea Norton (12)   68

Hartford High School
Stewart Cain (14)   68
Lisa Yould (12)   69
Claire Bagnall (15)   70
David Wood (12)   71
Katie Garner (15)   72
Laura Fuller (15)   73
Sophie Scott (12)   74
Lucy Washburn (12)   74
Zack Adlington (13)   75
Emily Godden (11)   75
Frances Clarke (12)   76
Sarah Reilly (12)   76
Chloe Carter (12)   77
Amy Sumner (12)   77
Amy Winnington (12)   78
Tom Whitehurst (11)   78
Kelly-Marie Towers (13)   79
Tom Blain (11)   79

Kirsty Sayle (13)	80
Zoe Lucock (11)	80
Georgia Bramhall (12)	81
Johanna Lawrence (12)	81
Hannah Crompton (12)	82
Zoe Lawrence (12)	82
Ashleigh Hopps (12)	83
Andrew Finemore (13)	83
Siobhan Eyes (15)	84
Sarah Dutton (13)	85
Claire Jones (12)	86
Maria Higson (13)	86
Amy Holehouse (12)	87
Lisa Noden (15)	87
Sophie Landreth (11)	88
Tom Mercer (12)	89
Emily Lindsay (12)	90
Martin Cadman (12)	90
Ed Hunt (14)	91
Rachel Ward (13)	91
Rachael Wilson (13)	92
Aaron Whalley (12)	92
Mark Parker (12)	93
Steven Moore (12)	93
Emily Birch (14)	94
Becky Walsh (12)	94
Sam Greenwood (16)	95
April Conway (14)	95
Katie Richardson (14)	96
Gareth Smith (13)	96
Laura Stafford (12)	97
Rachael Deakin (14)	97
Emma Sherwood (13)	98
Emily Pargeter (14)	98
Emma Beech (14)	99
Gareth Davies (14)	99
Rachel Bury (14)	100
Ben Yardley (12)	100

Neil Jacob (14)	128
Katie Shepherd (11)	128
Josh Thomson (12)	129
Jessica Scott (14)	129
Ben Stott (13)	130
Liam Edwards (13)	130
Callum Bayliss (11)	131
Megan Cain (11)	131
Lucy Widdowson (13)	132
Luke Hagan (13)	132
David Stevens (13)	132
David Jones (11)	133
Catriona Gilmour (14)	133
Jessica Houghton (12)	134
Kelly-Marie Tuff (14)	134
Sean Edwards (11)	135

Penketh High School

Claire Owen (15)	135

St Chad's RC High School, Runcorn

Jessica White (13)	136
Lisa Rimmer (14)	137
Jeni Reese (13)	138
Steffany White (14)	139
Chelscie Jones (13)	140
Nicola Roberts (13)	141
Rebecca Sargeant (13)	142
Courtney Reynolds (13)	143
Katie Page (13)	144
Alexandra Parkinson (13)	145
Natalie Sarsfield (13)	146
Erin Smith (13)	147
Hayley Meagher (13)	148
Laura Cliffe (13)	149
Laura Dixon (13)	150
Emma Cattrall (14)	151
Collette Davies (13)	152

The Poems

ORDERS OF THE DAY

'Get up!
Get washed!
Eat your breakfast!'
That's my mum,
She goes on and on and on and on . . .

'Sit down!
Shut up!
Get on with your work!'
That's my teacher,
She goes on and on and on and on . . .

'Play with me!
Carry me!
Listen to me!'
That's my younger cousin
He goes on and on and on and on . . .

'When's tea ready?
Bring it here!
Hey get off!'
That's me
I don't go on and on and on and on . . .

Do I?

Charlotte Bland (12)
Brine Leas High School

SCHOOL!

School,
Every kid's nightmare
But not this kid.
Johnny was a geek,
He loved school as much as his mum.

Lessons,
Some kids like lessons,
But not Paul,
He despised them,
He hated them more than girls.
(He hated them too)

Home time,
Is every kid's dream,
You can shout and scream as much as you want,
Until . . .

You go back tomorrow!

Tom Farr (13)
Brine Leas High School

THE GRAVESTONE

The gravestone
Spooky and wet
Get me out of here, I need a vet
The rain comes through the grass
Just like I'm in the bath
It's horrible and wet
Just wish you could see
How wet it is down here
For me.

Emily Jones (12)
Brine Leas High School

STILL WITH YOU

You may not know it,
But I'm still with you,
You may not see me,
But I'm still around you.

You may not hear me,
But I'm still talking to you,
You may not touch me,
But I'm always next to you.

You may not dream it,
But I'm always in your dreams,
You may not know it,
But I'm still with you.

I may not be in your mind,
But I'm in your heart.

Daniel Welch (13)
Brine Leas High School

BROTHERS

Brothers are very annoying
They put spiders in your mouth while you're yawning
Football, rollerblading, playing chess
Stealing my sweets, it's what they do best
At nights horns grow from their head
While we're all asleep in bed
They'll run out the house and scream out loud
I'm an annoying brother and very proud.

James McLean (13)
Brine Leas High School

JIMMY BORD

There was a boy called Jimmy Bord
Who thought it was good to play sports.
He ripped up paper and got his lucky snugby
Then there was the word *rugby!*

He went to the local club,
And his throat had a gulp.
Without the proper equipment,
He soon was in with a broken leg!

So back to the hat,
Looking like an 'old ugly rat',
He got his lucky . . . prawl,
and out was the name *Football!*

He went to the sports shop
With the clock tick tock,
Went to the local club
With shin pads and stuff.
Soon realised it's easy to get a black eye,
In hospital again two weeks on the trot,
And soon said, 'That's it I'll have to stop!'

Henry Richardson (12)
Brine Leas High School

SCHOOL!

School is a thing that comes five days a week,
For kids it is hell, something quite bleak.
School is a thing that everyone dreads,
Kids attention hangs by a thread.
School is tedious.

School is a thing with very little break,
Kids wish there were more to make.
School is a thing with many, many rules,
Kids stick to them like the crown jewels.
School is tiresome.

But wait . . .

School is a thing which helps you learn,
School is a thing you don't want to burn.
School is a thing which gets you friends,
School is a thing with very little bends.
School is . . . OK.

School is a thing which teaches you manners,
School is a thing which is just a taster.
School is a thing which keeps you fit,
School isn't just one big pit.
School I suppose is all right after all.

Daniel Grant (13)
Brine Leas High School

I'M STILL HERE

I have only gone round the corner
To a different place.
But in your heart I will always stay.

Please don't cry for me cause really I'm still here.

When you hear the wind whistling
You can be sure that it's always me.

Wherever you go I will follow you,
In the day and in the night.
No matter what, I'm sure to be always by your side.

Even though I'm invisible,
It's me you can hear.
Please don't have fear with me, still being here.

Natalie Tomkins (13)
Brine Leas High School

I'VE LOST MY MIND

I've lost my mind it's right
I don't know my left from my right.

I am turning into a mouse (well I think I am)
They say I should be in a loopy house.

I've lost my mind it's correct
I just had my tea for my break

I'm going mad I know I am
I just fed the dog a jar of jam.

Christopher Beswick (12)
Brine Leas High School

I Don't Know Why

I'm the tallest in my class
and I don't know why.

People just ignore me
and I don't know why.

People kick me
and I don't know why.

I always put my hand up to answer
questions in class
but the teacher never looks at me
and I don't know why.

The only way I'm different is
I'm black not white.

Laura Hollinshead (12)
Brine Leas High School

The Red Red Rose

The red, red rose
grows in the summer.

It smells like the heavenly Heaven
so now is your chance to get some
to keep this smell forever.

The colours are bright and beautiful
and your eyes get pulled towards it.

So take good care of those flowers
and they'll be there with you forever.

Luke Billington (12)
Brine Leas High School

MAKE ME HAPPY AGAIN

Another day has gone,
and you still have not come back.
Do you know how much I miss you?
I'm living without hope and doubt.

Thinking about you every day,
every minute, every second.
Just longing that you're with me!

My life is so boring,
now that you have gone.
Won't you just come back to me?
Whether it's just for one more day.

Just make me happy again!

Lauren Lockhart (13)
Brine Leas High School

THE BIG ONE

The rugby World Cup is coming soon
Will Italy get the wooden spoon?

Is Wilko going to get more points
And will South Africa break more joints?

Ask yourself will England win
Or will Australia chuck us in the bin?

Is it going to be the day
That we make Australia really pay?

Henry Hackett (12)
Brine Leas High School

IF ONLY

If you were a sickness
and I was a cure
maybe I would love you forever more.

If you were a weed
and I was a flower
maybe I would think of you every minute on the hour.

If you were young,
and I was old
maybe we would be together even in the cold.

If you were crowded
and I was alone
maybe I'd stop ringing you on the phone.

If you were the ground
and I was the rain
perhaps people would stop calling me insane.

Emily Cadwallader (12)
Brine Leas High School

THE ANGEL OF DARKNESS

He glides the night on wings unheard,
With eyes that see as clear as day,
Silent death to his prey he brings,
With talons of steel that none can break,
Yet gentle as a summer's breeze,
As to his young their food he brings,
Again once more,
He soon takes flight,
Angel of Darkness, master of the night.

Keith Massey (12)
Brine Leas High School

THE TREE

I don't see,
I don't speak,
But I listen,
I listen to everything that's said.

I stand at the bottom of the garden,
I stand there all day and all night,
People don't know that I'm listening,
But I take in everything that's said.

I don't see,
I don't speak,
But I'm listening.

I'm listening to everything that's said.

Laura Gerrard (12)
Brine Leas High School

DIFFERENT THINGS

My teacher is very tall,
    But I am very small,
        It is not fair, I gave you a dare to go
and kiss his little bear.
    Here is a butterfly, flying with his
rainbow wings of colours.
    Here is the rain trickling into the river.
    There is a little bat flying through the jungle,
sees a little tiny buzzy bee.
        Books are beautiful, beautiful as bees.

Kelly Lewis (12)
Brine Leas High School

MY DAD AND HIS DAY

My dad's work says he's always late,
He looks so smart I think he's on a date,
I explained I drew a horse and cart,
And baked a lovely blueberry tart.

But he doesn't listen to boring old me,
I don't want to make him a cup of tea,
He can also have his dinner cold,
Lots of cheese, with loads of mould.

But instead of ignoring me,
He fills my heart with lots of glee,
'Do you want to go bowling today?'
'Yes I do, hip hip hooray.'

The day was late and I was tired,
There was this boy I really admired,
Tomorrow will be a busy day,
Me and my dad will have lots to say.

Today as I stepped through the door,
I had noticed a scrubby floor,
I finally got the toy I desired,
As my old folk had been fired.

I wish this day was never born,
When I got up at cracker dawn,
I felt so sorry for my dad,
For the long awful day he's had.

Danniella Ingram (12)
Brine Leas High School

SEEING THE LIGHT

The clouds were white,
The sky was blue,
The sun was bright,
I saw the light.
Not knowing he was round the corner,
Not knowing, not thinking, not hoping,
Not wishing, not praying,
But believing.
My love for him was slowly fading
I see his face, his messed up hair,
His dirty clothes,
But she is not there.
Don't go to him, I say to myself,
Don't take his useless lies, don't cry for him.
Let him go
Let him know
Wait, just walk,
No need to face him,
Just walk.

Katy Vaughan (14)
Brine Leas High School

THE DAY MY NAN DIED

The day that my nan died,
I cried and cried and cried,
I really hated the sight and it gave me a fright,
I couldn't sleep all night because of that fright,
I still miss her but she will always be in my heart!

Siobhan Smith (11)
Brine Leas High School

CHOCOLATE

Chocolate, chocolate, chocolate.
It's brown and yummy it fills your tummy
It's also white as bright as a light.

Birthdays, Christmas and Easter too.
Something to eat from me to you.
When you're down it cheers you up
You can even drink it out of a cup.

Chocolate comes in different flavours,
Just for people with different behaviours.
It's a present for every occasion
For boys and girls, grandparents too.
Even for parents if you want to.

Scott Maude (13)
Brine Leas High School

JACOB

My friend is Jacob, black and sad,
He is the same as you.
He can cry and laugh,
He is Jacob, black and worried.
You say things about him,
To hurt and wound,
He is Jacob black and depressed.
Each morning he wakes up,
Feeling scared and apprehensive,
Thinking of what people will say next.
He is Jacob black and angry,
He is strong and will take the pain,
I don't blame him for his anger,
He is Jacob, black and proud.

Joshua Ruane (12)
Brine Leas High School

MOTHER

My mum is my star, my big shining star.
She keeps me on my feet, she never lets me fall.
Deep down in our hearts, we'll never be apart.

My star is my guide, my one and only guide.
That star is my friend, my only true friend.
That star is my mum, she shines like the sun.

She has a heart of gold, she never lets me go cold.
The sun is my life, the sun is a star.
My mum is that sun, she's also that star.

My mum will care for me, whether I'm fit or ill.
She will even die for me, she will go for the kill.
I will die for her, I will cry for her.

When I'm with my mum, we have some fun.
We act like adults, we can also act like clowns.
We have our ups, we have our downs.

Rebecca Clutton (13)
Brine Leas High School

THE CAT

The cat on the doorstep sat so still,
Black and sleek,
Just a flick of whisker, a blink of eye,
So people know he isn't asleep,
I shut my window with a bang!
A flutter of wings, a cloud of dust,
He gave me such a look of disgust
As he stalked away majestically
He decided to try another day!

Lucy Davenport (13)
Brine Leas High School

THE REDCOATS

Redcoats,
The British infantry,
Marching to their death,
Fed to the cannons,
Assaulting the breach,
Fighting for their country,
Dying for their country.

They once won at Gawilghur,
Then later at Badajoz,
Nothing will stop them,
They are the invincible army,
Their enemies fear them,
Their commanders are proud of them,
They are the redcoats.

Muskets and bayonets,
Shrapnel and mines,
Explosions from cannon fire,
Sabres and claymores,
Steel upon steel,
Man killing man,
They are the redcoats.

They march into cannon fire,
March to their death,
Slaughter the enemy,
They are the redcoats,
Pillaging, plundering, raping,
They are the redcoats,
They are *our* soldiers.

Andrew Down (13)
Brine Leas High School

A SCENT OF SUMMER

The most favourite of course is the English rose,
It's so elegant, pretty and neat.
There's so many different varieties,
But all will smell as sweet.

The second is the lily,
It's so radiant, large and bright.
They only grow in the summer months,
As they go forth towards the light.

The third is the poppy,
With its vibrant colour red.
The blooms only last for a day or two,
And then the petals start to shed.

Elizabeth Johnson (13)
Brine Leas High School

NIGHT

The sky goes dark and filled with stars,
Beneath travel a few scattered cars.
Owls hooting, bats flying,
Mice squeaking, dogs crying.
In the streets, out come the rats,
Followed by the night-crawling cats.

Headlights provide the only glimpse of light,
The stars above shine so bright.
People sleeping in their beds,
'I don't like the dark,' the little boy said.
Doors locked, the house is secure,
We all want to sleep a little bit more.

Yasmin Preston (13)
Brine Leas High School

A BOOK NEVER ENDS

The depth of a book is endless,
Like the sky it never ends.
Taking you from world to world,
Dimension to dimension,
A book never ends.

They free your mind
And inspire all you do
You get lost in an imaginary world,
Seeking for more,
A book never ends.

Flicking through each and every page,
A puzzle being built.
Each and every character
Your new best friend or foe.
A book never ends.

When the plot has thickened
And the mystery solved.
The characters gone back to bed,
Until it's read again.
You never forget a story
For it's endless in your brain.

Ashley Yarwood (13)
Brine Leas High School

A Journey Down The Black Slope

I feel the chairlift,
Hit the back of my legs,
It pushes me off,
I ski away.

I arrive at the top,
Of the black slope,
It scares me but,
I ski away.

My heart pounds,
It's an icy turn,
My life is in danger,
I ski away.

My biggest fear,
I lose control,
My thighs ache,
I ski away.

My poles sink,
Into the snow,
But I don't show fear,
As my journey ends here.

Natalie Dodd (13)
Brine Leas High School

THE NIGHT

The night is cold and lonely,
Nothing is undisturbed,
The night is a cave of darkness,
Yet nothing more than sky,
The screeching of owls,
And wailing of wolves,
Leaves nothing undisturbed,
But yet there is just one place,
That doesn't stir at night,
It isn't a bird at flight,
Nor a plant under light.

The night is cold and dark,
Nothing is left untouched,
The night is a hole of darkness,
Yet nothing more than sky,
The moaning of trees,
And rustling of leaves,
Leaves nothing left untouched,
But yet there is just one place,
That doesn't stir at night,
It is not a flying kite,
Nor a rabbit in a fight.

But this one place is bigger than all,
But still it does not stir,
This one place could only be . . .
. . . *The sky!*

Penny O'Reilly (13)
Brine Leas High School

MY SCRAPBOOK!

My scrapbook has many pictures in it
My mum has threatened to bin it.

I like to keep it by my bed
Because there's things in it that people have said.

There are people in it that I've loved and lost
And there are people in it that send me post.

There are pictures of me when I was chubby
And pictures of me standing by my cubby.

There are entries I've written about a dream
When I crossed a big old stream.

There are pictures of me with my friends
And memories of holidays that will never end.

There are pictures of my brother and me
And a picture of the Mediterranean Sea.

One picture is of my cat
And the other is of my mum's favourite hat.

There's one of my dad when he was young
And one of my cousin who has a very long tongue.

There is a picture of the bee that gave me a lump
And a picture of me when I had a bit of a bump.

Many memories I have stored
In my scrapbook when I was bored.

Joanne Knight (13)
Brine Leas High School

NANTWICH TOWN

Nantwich Town shines like a crown,
That's the pub's name, it makes people frown,
River Weaver gleaming brown,
Life's like a box of chocolates
living in Nantwich Town.

I hear children laughing with glee,
I see women on a shopping spree,
I hear people shouting at me,
Life's a box of chocolates
living in Nantwich Town.

There's lots to do,
Such as playing peekaboo,
Or gather your mates and go to the pool,
Life's a box of chocolates
living in Nantwich Town.

Autumn arrives, down falls the leaves,
They play to the wind's fun games
Flying and swirling
Life's a box of chocolates
living in Nantwich Town.

Finally I end this poem about my town,
Leaning back smiling proud,
Nantwich Town really does shine
like a crown.

Craig Wright (13)
Brine Leas High School

WAITING

Tears of gold fall down her face
She wears a dress all made of lace
As she cries the thunder roars
Her face so soft, as her tears fall
She stands alone in the bright moonlight
Until she catches that one sight
There she will stand always watching and waiting
She tries so hard to calm her hating
As she stands, awaiting his return.
Her love for him will always burn.
He went away to find his wealth
And left one winter's night with stealth
To earn his fortune and his bride
So they could live together side by side.
What she does not know, is that on his way
A tragic accident would leave her feeling betrayed.
He lies so still barely breathing
As the darkness of the night comes weaving.
His ship now lies beneath the waves
And it seems only he is saved
And there she stands upon the shore
Where she will wait forever more
For her true love who never returned.
Yet her love for him will always burn.

Laura Maddocks (13)
Brine Leas High School

In The Graveyard . . .

In the graveyard it's quiet during the day.
But just you wait until the night.
Moonlight, stars and lots of creepy graves
When the moon is at its highest,
The graves come alive.

Zombies, bats and lots of skeletons,
You wouldn't like to be here when it happens.
Little children who shouldn't have died
And ghosts of old people who have passed away.
Scary things happen during the night.

Scary faces which look like Hallowe'en masks
With massive white eyes which stare at you.
Bushes of thorns with red dying roses,
A big lawn of muddy grass,
And large black birds circling the yards.

As the moon goes down, things settle down,
Zombies and skeletons go back into their graves.
Bats fly away and roses come back alive,
The moon is nowhere to be seen.
The graveyard is silent again.

Robyn O'Reilly (13)
Brine Leas High School

I JUST CAN'T CHOOSE

Cats can be big,
Cats can be small,
Cats can be short
And cats can be tall.

Some are black,
Some are white,
Some are dull
And some are bright.

We feed them cat food,
But they prefer mice,
They chase them; catch them,
Then eat them, mmmm nice.

Some are boring,
Some are crazy,
Some are active,
But most are just lazy.

Some are Tabbies,
Then there's Maine Coons,
Persians, Tortoiseshells,
I just can't choose.

Fiona Lowe (13)
Brine Leas High School

ELEPHANTS

Elephants are big
Elephants are grey
They walk round the jungle
For the whole of the day.

They store lots of stuff into their minds
So they never forget anything
Their trunks can be used to get food
As well as for a swing.

Elephants can be big
Elephants can be tall
Most of the time they're massive
But when they're newborn they're small.

They can't be found everywhere
Even though I wish they could
They live in Africa and Asia
and they bathe in the mud.

Made out of clay, wood and plastic
Elephant toys are found everywhere
Ornaments, calendars, cuddly toys
Wherever you go, elephants are there.

Alexandra Holmes (13)
Brine Leas High School

THE WEATHER

The weather is always changing,
it's always hot or cold.
The sun is shining in the sky,
the stars will twinkle in the night.

You get big rain clouds,
and dense fog.
Piles of snow,
and buckets of sleet.

Clouds of mist,
and heavy rain.
No one likes these,
as they spoil your fun!

Fun in the sun,
that's what we all want,
Lying on beaches,
getting a tan!

You cannot change the weather,
no one ever can.
It will do as it pleases,
no matter whatever you do!

Sam Cliffe (13)
Brine Leas High School

FRIENDS AND FAMILIES

They're always looking out for us,
Sometimes when we don't even ask them to,
They're forever looking after us and working out our problems.

They don't like it when we are sad,
And are always grateful when we are happy,
But care for us when we are feeling down.

Our best friends are always there for us,
Through all the problems in our life,
Good or bad they don't mind, as long as we're okay.

Through everything that happens,
Our friends are always there for us,
No matter what they are, a person, pet or plant.

Our families don't always understand why we are how we are,
And may sometimes stop us from doing what we want,
They always say that they know best, and we will understand one day.

But they're always there when we need them most,
I don't know how we could live without them,
Even though we may fight sometimes, we never seem to part.

Sometimes we might lose someone close to us,
But they're always in our hearts.
Their smiling faces always cheer us up,
So just think how lucky we are.

Harriet Davies (13)
Brine Leas High School

MAKES YOU WANT TO CRY

There were three men in a war, each of them will die
It's so sad it makes you want to cry.

The first got a gun,
And started shooting like it was fun
One of them was shot down dead
The bullet pierced straight through his head.
It's so sad it makes you want to cry.

The second man was up in flight
And luckily to his delight
He killed so many
Of the enemy
But then to his dismay
He sadly passed away.
It's so sad it makes you want to cry.

The third man's story, now his was tragic
His death was as quick as magic
It was a bomb you see, a bomb that fell
A bomb that made him go down to Hell
You see the bomb blew up in his face
Leaving not even a trace.
It's so sad it makes you want to cry.

Now all three men
Are in Heaven
Yes each are in a happy place in the sky.
It's so sad it makes you want to cry.

Craig Morris (12)
Brine Leas High School

A LIFE AT WAR

I never thought that the day would come,
To depart from my family which should not be done.

Another day in the trenches,
Watching, waiting for the signal to go.

Sound of gun's echo in my ear,
The thought of family brought me tears.

Sitting there everyday not moving a muscle,
People dropping bombs ahead, so much hustle and bustle.

I was a team of seven now a team of four,
We four are still standing yet three lie on the floor.

The sun starts to set and us four are still here,
Tonight we are alive on this big blue sphere.

War kills millions of people but millions are still alive.
Tomorrow will be different another million may die.

Every day a new day starts,
The same routine but hopefully us four will not part.

It's been five months since we started fighting in this war,
We've all forgotten what life was like before.

There is a long way to go and a lot of hard work,
But hopefully one day peace will rule the world.

Chevaune Halewood (13)
Brine Leas High School

MY FRIEND

What to do and what to say are totally different things,
And where to go and when to go, I go without knowing,
How such of a little thing can bring such great beginning.

No bigger than a rock, I think it's kind of fun,
How all that it really needs is the rain and sun.
It may be big, it may be small,
It may rise above the rest if it's really tall.

I like its rough touch, I like its strong feel,
It burrows deep underground to find its watery meal.
It listens, it's wise and very strong,
It's been around a hundred years long.

I think it's mine, if it were a him,
I'd talk and talk, if talkings not a sin.
He's no one else's, he's my best friend,
He's no one else's, he's mine to the end.

For my friend, he's a tree,
He never talks, only listens.
In the wind he slowly whispers,
Now you see who it is,
He's a tree, he's my friend,
I think I'll build a treehouse in the end.

Ben Marshall (13)
Brine Leas High School

WAR

Suicide bombers, soldiers killed,
Is all we hear on the news.
Families flee, away from homes,
For a chance to save their lives.

Soldiers move in to keep the peace,
But peace will not be kept.
For round the corner a terrorist stands,
With explosives strapped to his chest.

Bloodstained doors and wounded men,
Are all that can be seen.
Broken guns and blown up cars,
And glass scattered everywhere.

Crying babies, children scared,
Wondering what's going on.
Hiding and waiting for it to stop,
But the war just keeps going on.

Months go by and thousands are killed,
The news says the war has stopped.
But for the people who live there, it's just begun,
Devastation will haunt them for good.

Daniel Walsh (13)
Brine Leas High School

To Die At The Drop Of A Hat

Streets paved with people as the rush hour traffic starts.
Busses passing.
Teenagers walking to school.
Little they know, many tears they will shed,
as people die at the drop of a hat.
All this pain from one idea, but living life is yet so near!
People living, people laughing, parliament speaking, taxis running,
planes flying overhead,
but people will die at the drop of a hat.
So quick life is given and just so as it's taken.
A cry of pain as an old man is blown away.
A café explodes after a final three-second-tick tock of a clock in a car.
A family apart.
A one minute silence for the normal life livers of the streets.
So much madness is here in this head of this man.
He awakens from his plan
his 'silk smooth' idea will bring so much pain.
Ashamed he is that he is capable of thinking a thought where people
die at the drop of *his* hat.

Dan Johnson (13)
Brine Leas High School

My Dog

The cute little face of a Border collie,
Her eyes so bright, her black fur so dark.
Being with her is a pleasure.
She plays all day long and sleeps all night.
She likes to be outside and chase the birds.
Also she likes to bark very loud,
She is very good though.
She is my dog.

Hannah Butler (11)
Brine Leas High School

AND SHE WAS GONE

The sun shines brightly in the cloudy blue sky,
While a rejected girl walks quietly by,
She walks along high streets, getting drunk by beer,
Wondering what it would be like to disappear.

She wonders and wonders, and thinks why she's here,
She thinks it would be better to disappear.

She carries on walking and thinking, still
While the cold breeze gives her a chill.
She feels lonely and heartless and dead,
Wondering, if she'd be better off in an everlasting bed.

She wonders and wonders and thinks why she's here,
She thinks it would be better to disappear.

But she does not know what's coming her way,
Neither does she know what's going to happen
The next day,
She still feels lonely and heartless and dead,
Maybe she should find an everlasting bed.

She wonders and wonders and thinks why she's here,
She knows it would be better to disappear.

The sun shone brightly in the cloudy blue sky,
As the disappearing girl walked quietly by,
She once walked along, the high Street, getting drunk on beer,
But now she knows what it's like to disappear.

Bryony Page (12)
Brine Leas High School

RIVERS

Rivers start at a source
Far away from the sea,
Then they form a trickle,
Heading towards the sea.

They trickle down mountains,
And onto the hills,
Where they pick up sand,
Heading towards the sea.

They form a stream,
Going over rocks with rapids,
And make their own path,
Heading towards the sea.

Finally they form rivers,
Flowing slowly and gracefully,
Sweeping around corners depositing sand,
Heading towards the sea.

Then they reach the sea,
Sometimes they form a delta,
Sometimes they make a mouth,
But whatever happens they always reach the sea.

Matthew Brooks (13)
Brine Leas High School

ME AND MY BEST FRIEND

Me and my best friend,
We go everywhere together,
Even to the supermarket,
Even to my gran's,
She takes me to her nan's,
We go everywhere together!

Her eyelashes are as thick and as long
                          as a giraffe's neck,
Her skin is as soft as her hair,
She has big blue eyes that glow in the dark,
She is like a princess!

She wears the coolest clothes,
But I choose them for her,
We wear the same clothes,
We think it looks cool!

We do the same things,
We have the same habits,
She likes dancing,
So do I,
There's only one problem, my best friend is I!

Janine Isherwood (13)
Brine Leas High School

ONE PERFORMANCE

A dark quiet hall with silent, still faces,
Moving footsteps are heard in the large open spaces.
I walk slowly on the stage.
As my fellow dancers disappear,
The bright lights are switched on,
The spotlight is pointing at me,
I am for the first time seen clearly.
The music starts, I look ahead.
There are butterflies in my stomach,
All the blood rushes to my head.
My mind has gone blank, I feel the rhythm inside,
I cannot see the audience in front of me
And the routine comes to life.
I do not know how and I do not know why,
But I am unaware of how quickly time passes by,
And finally, once again, I see a dark, quiet hall
And silent still faces.
Moving footsteps are heard fading away.

Charlotte Clapham *(13)*
Brine Leas High School

THE CREATURE

Its shadow crawls across the bathroom door
Moving through the dark, open spaces
Its green eyes flicker in the moonlight
Nearer and nearer it goes
But, it stops
Everything is quiet
The earth stands still
It opens its mouth,
And . . .

Chris Board *(12)*
Brine Leas High School

LABELS

People today wear many designs
To show that they have different minds
Some include a tracksuit and *Nike*
So people think you want a fight.

Things may vary from time to time
To show that you are worth a dime
Like *Levis, Vans* or *Adidas*
Cuz then you feel you've got the class.

Before you spend lots of money
On very expensive things
Just remember these are life's
Very little things.

Tom Smith (13)
Brine Leas High School

BEST FRIENDS!

Best friends, best friends
They're always there when you feel down,
But when you do something stupid
They make you feel a right clown.

Best friends, best friends,
If something is wrong,
And you don't know what to do,
They're always there and help to comfort you.

Best friends, best friends,
You'll probably know them for the rest of your life,
Even though sometimes
You could stab them with a knife.

Simon Berresford (13)
Brine Leas High School

ANIMALS, ANIMALS

Animals, animals everywhere
can you see the polar bear?
Animals, animals everywhere
can you hear the barn owl singing?
Animals, animals everywhere
can you see the monkey swinging?
Animals, animals everywhere
can you hear a baby bird singing?
Animals, animals everywhere
can you see a grizzly bear?
Animals, animals everywhere
can you hear the robin singing his song?
Animals, animals everywhere
can you see an elephant?
Animals, animals everywhere
can you hear the dog howling?
Animals, animals everywhere
There's no more to spare.

John Morris (14)
Brine Leas High School

EARTH

Before the beginning I was there,
Fast running rivers and fresh clean air.
For millions and millions of years,
Animals roamed without any fears.
Powerful winds and turbulent seas,
Lush green grass and strong tall trees.
This was me in God's creation,
This is me now, a human devastation.

My lungs are filled with ash and smoke,
My heart from drilling oil is almost broke.
My face is scarred from toil and war,
I'm screaming and screaming, 'Please, no more.'
What is it that they cannot see?
They're hurting themselves they're hurting me.
My forest burnt my oil drained,
Tell me then what have they gained?

But when the humans have died out,
I'll still be here without a doubt.
Slowly healing through eons of time,
I will be rid of this evil crime.

Eve Kirby (12)
Brine Leas High School

MY FAMILY

My dad can be sometimes sarcastic
but most of the time he's fantastic,
gives me pocket money,
tells jokes that are funny
and he's a car racing fanatic.

Now Jill is the name of my mum,
and sometimes she acts kinda dumb
she cooks all my meals
shops for all the best deals
when I'm naughty she gets really glum.

I have a young brother called James
who is just a bit short on brains
he makes lots of noise
like most little boys
and then goes and plays with his trains.

My dog Jet is incredibly bright
I think she must have second sight
she can bury a bone
always finds her way home
and really gives burglars a fright.

Nicole Jones (12)
Brine Leas High School

THE LITERAL CHILD

I don't understand.
They tell me to do it, so I do.
They say, 'I don't want to hear another word out of you!'
So I didn't.
I didn't speak for three days.
Then they yelled.

I don't understand.
They tell me to do it, so I do.
They say, 'Go and stand in the corner and don't move!'
So I didn't.
I didn't move till home time,
Then they yelled.

I don't understand.
They tell me to do it, so I do.
They say, 'Draw a table in your books, now!'
So I did.
It was lovely, 3D, made of oak. I had the wood grain effect just right.
Then they yelled.

Why is life so complicated?

Charlotte Bridges (12)
Brine Leas High School

My Best Friend!

She has a lot of beauty
you can see it in her face,
and she's bubbly and fruity.

She's so sweet
I love her to bits,
She's someone you really need to meet.

We are closer than close, yes we are
She's like my big sister
She's a shining star.

We do everything together
She's a wicked mate,
We are like birds of a feather.

Nikki!

Kelsey Cadwallader (13)
Brine Leas High School

Best Friends

B   est friends, me and Heather
E   very day we chatter away
S   itting down forever, and ever,
T   alking no matter what time of day.

F   riends are always there
R   eal friends like me best
I   ndeed are not like the rest
E   very day is so fab
N   ot very often are they bad
D   on't you see that this is why
S   he's my best mate, her and I.

Katie Berresford (13)
Brine Leas High School

DEATH

When I die, do not cry,
Do not despair, I will always be there,
I am a ghost following you around,
I know what you are doing,
Thinking and saying,
Remember me for who I really was,
And listen carefully,
Because
I am in the wind, in your heart and soul,
Forever and always,
Until the rest of your days.
Do not cry,
I did not die.

Sophie McKinnon (12)
Brine Leas High School

SCHOOL

I went in with a squash
My friends walked in rather posh
We sat and ate our lunch
In a rather big bunch.

We talked about our day
And I was just about to say!
When the bell went again . . .
'The bell is a pain.'

My friends went to form
The room was very warm
We went to next lesson
A whole class *detention!*

Verity Baxter (12)
Brine Leas High School

THE VOICES OF THE FOES

We march on towards that snow-white hill.
We lay in ambush just waiting.
I grip my weapon ready to fight these angry beasts.
The order's given, the peace is broken and replaced by shouts and
gunfire.
I look down my barrel and see not a beast but a normal man, sad, hurt
and lost.
I glance around and see masses of corpses lying there and wonder what
brought this on.
My eye meets his and he raises his gun but drops it,
I drop mine look around and begin to weep for my fellow man now
staining the scenery.
I hear a shot and a soft thud, I gasp a short sharp breath.
I see the bullet hit and run towards him, my enemy dying I cry for a
man that I don't know.
My last memory, the voice of my foe.

Stephen Crow (12)
Brine Leas High School

THE SLAVE

So this is my life enslaved by my parents
They're always nagging, telling and '*ad-vis-ing*'
I hope I'm not going to be like that when I'm older
Plus when you answer back their face goes mad and reddens.

It's not my fault that I whine
It's only my mum and dad who say they didn't in their youth
I hate it when they hide stuff and not tell us what they're doing
I wonder what it would be like if we knew the truth.

Yesterday they asked me to clean my bedroom so I said, '*No.*'
They grounded me for a week so what did I do?
I sat in my bedroom till the mess was knee-high
But then Mum came in and shouted, '*Why?*'

So when I'm older I'm going to feed my kids sweets, snacks and
chocolate
I'm not going to order them to clean the dishes, cars and the toilet
So when I'm older and have a spoilt little brat
Oh sod it, they treated me badly, so I'll do just that.

Jack Marshall (14)
Brine Leas High School

SWEETS

If I were made of candy,
I wonder what I'd be.
I could be soft
like a marshmallow,
Or smooth like chocolate.
I could be crunchy
like honeycomb pieces,
or sour like Haribo Tangfastics.
I could be bubbly
like a bar of Aero,
or round like Polos.
I could be fresh like a Tic Tac
Or hard like a gobstopper.
I could be colourful
like liquorice allsorts,
or chewy like bubblegum.
I could be as cold as ice cream,
or hollow like Kinder eggs.
I could be long like strawberry laces,
or as sparkly as moondust.
I could be in a world of my own
like a bar of Cadbury Dream,
or stretchy like caramel.
I could be sugary like rock,
or breakable like Kit Kat.
I would choose to be all of them!

Amanda Kingdom (12)
Brine Leas High School

COMA

Waking up now I see
People looking staring right through me
Wonder what happened
What was not meant to be.

And suddenly I'm in my own world
Coma
Don't know the difference between a boy and a girl
Coma
Where did all the money go
What happened to it?
There's a needle in my vein injecting fluid.

Was I a good man or was I bad?
Did I have a wife?
Was I a dad?
Coma.
People are talking now
What are they saying?
Can't quite make out the words
Hope they ain't praying.

My legs aren't moving now
I'm in trouble want to get out of here
Out on the double.

White light shining in my eyes
The sort that's so blinding it'll make you cry
Coma.

James Murphy (13)
Brine Leas High School

I HAVE A LITTLE SISTER

I have a little sister that always follows me
And what can be the use of her is more than I see.
When my parents told me about her, I said, 'How surely can this be?
How possibly can they have one as intelligent as me?'

She gets loads of presents, but seems to chew them up
I think she's taking lessons from Cocoa, our little pup.
Does she not understand that she's a baby not a dog
Or is her brain so small it's smaller than a frog's?

I also can't believe that she sleeps through all the day
And when it comes to night I hear Mummy say,
'Go to sleep, little one, in the heat of the fire'
Does she not understand or is she some sort of vampire?

I told my mummy today I think my sister's dumb and hasn't got a brain
But she just smiled at me and said, 'Darling, you were just the same!'

Ashleigh Henderson (13)
Brine Leas High School

CAFC

C   rewe are my team I shout and roar
R   ich Walker and Dean Ashton always score
E   ach player all set and ready to go
W   e shout, 'Come on Alex let's give 'em a blow!'
E   ach and every chance they had.

A   lex players made the opposition mad
L   eft to right they tried to score
E   ach player not wanting to have a draw
X   tra time in the end - we won and several goals we had!

Joseph Wood (11)
Brine Leas High School

IF ONLY

If only life was as great
as a butterfly is beautiful.

If only life was as clear,
as the night sky sparkles.

If only . . .

If only life was as happy
as a naked flame is bright.

If only life is as wonderful
as a newly opened rose is pretty.

If only . . .

If life was always tranquil
would we appreciate life at all?

Helen Russell (12)
Brine Leas High School

ALLEY CAT

Slinking, winding grass
Sneaky alley cat passed
Jumping branches, sniffing food
He thought he was a bit of a dude.
Slinking, winding grass
Sneaky alley cat passed
The sneaky tom realised
His prey was gone
Up on the roof singing.
Slinking, winding grass,
Sneaky alley cat pass . . .

Ellis Warke (11)
Brine Leas High School

THE WORLD AND ITS WAR

The war is a thing that will never end,
There is always a beginning but never an end,
There was World War I which Britain won.
Now the war in Iraq is almost done.
All the pain and suffering will be gone
Many people died, few survived.
Many are still rebuilding their lives.

The war in Iraq caused tears of pain
Which would make the families go insane
For the loss of their loved ones which caused mighty shame,
Upon this war which left people in dismay.

Who will win the war? No one knows
Thank god it's not us fighting out there alone.
All we can do is bless the souls of those fighting out there
                                    on their own.

God bless.

Jessica Mair (13)
Brine Leas High School

CORNWALL

This is a place I like to go every summer
With places like Newquay, Padstow and St Ives
There are plenty of places to spend my money
From things like bracelets and rings to surfboards and shoes.
When the sun is shining it's even better
As I love to sit and soak up the sun.

Now the beach is just as good!
With the clear blue sea and the soft golden sand
I can sit, swim and surf
Taking the dog along the shore, up and down the seafront
The tide's coming in better get back before it comes right up!

Back in the car on my way back to the caravan site
I'm deciding whether I might
Go for a wander around the caravan site
But as I get back to the van it's turning dark
So I settle down and decide to watch 'The Sixth Sense'.

With this being my last day
I decide to shop again
Buying bags and shoes, clothes and jewellery
I really have made the best of my last day!

Lauren Taylor (13)
Brine Leas High School

THE CAT SAT ON THE DIRTY MAT

My cat sat on a dirty mat,
He would not move, he didn't care,
But why? It was covered in rabbit hair,
He sat there for hours, he wouldn't budge,
Even when I gave him a nudge.
I told him, 'Besmond you need to move,
Here, go on have some food,
Please, don't be rude, come on have some food!
Look here, I said, if you won't come
I'll smack your bum!'
And so I did, but he ran and hit the bin lid,
He was really hurt, so I placed him on my skirt
And said, 'I am sorry, I love you Bezz!'

Natalie Oldershaw (11)
Brine Leas High School

THE FAILED KING

There was once a king on a golden throne,
His palace was made of fine cut stone.
Then one day he became grey,
His son had died and he sat in dismay.
What could he do? It came so soon
It only happened that afternoon.

A year or two past,
But not very fast.
The king was a fraud,
He failed his task.
To produce a son, to rule in his stead,
But it was too late for the king was dead.

Steven Loasby (13)
Brine Leas High School

MY NEW TEACHER

My maths teacher
She tends to scare,
But even worse,
She always stares.

Mr Young
My tech teacher,
Acts a bit strange,
Turns out he's a preacher.

There's a teacher here,
Called Miss Cuddily.
She jots about a bit,
Always needs a wee.

A teacher here's got
No fashion sense
And always is
Very tense.

Miss Spencer
Thrives caffeine
And sometimes,
Can be very mean.

I can't believe
Miss Manley's like that,
Always moaning
About her cat.

If you think
The teachers are mad
You should meet my mates
They're even bad.

Jo Stockton (11)
Brine Leas High School

BEST FRIENDS, SOPHIE AND I

She's my best friend and I'm hers too
We have other friends of course we do
But she says, 'There's nothing like me and you.'
Best friends, Sophie and I.

We go shopping at the weekend
Think of all the money we would spend
We know our friendship will never end
Best friends, Sophie and I.

When she's gone I always miss her
We always look good in a picture
Natural friends, me and her
Best friend, Sophie and I.

Sadly in the end we grow apart
There's always a place for her in my heart
But we will always be, you and me
Best friend, Sophie and I.

Joanna Thelwell (13)
Brine Leas High School

THE GRUESOME GREEKS

The gruesome Greeks, they were a bunch
Icarus fell into the sea with a splash
The tale was told that Theseus was dead
When in fact he'd chopped off the Minotaur's head.
Jason led the Argonauts to glory
But his adventures were positively gory.
Zeus got an axe through his head
Instead of his brain Athena popped out instead.
Everyone hailed Xerxe's reign
Until his army went down the drain.
Spartans were the toughest fighters
They carried no guns, whips or lighters.
The Trojan Horse was a magnificent plan
But they destroyed the enemy down to the last man.
Nartese got into one of his moods
So the gods got angry and were not amused.
The wars were violent and bloody
But all the soldiers got muddy.
The Spartan's hair was long
They cut off the enemies' tongues.

Ben Smith (11)
Brine Leas High School

THE WASHING MACHINE ATE MY UNDERPANTS!

(Well to make me sound like I'm not that crazy,
I blamed it on my baby puppy)

One boring afternoon,
I phoned a friend for town.

I thought *what should I wear?*
I put pants on and found my flairs.

After shopping I put my pants in the washer,
I put them in there because it's a super washer.

I went to get my pants out,
They weren't there so I looked about.

My friend was coming, 'Oh what shall I do?'
My friend came in and shouted '*Boo!*'

I realised where my pants had gone,
I found out by my brother Don.

My washing machine was hungry, it ate my favourite pants all up,
Also it had eaten my mother's wedding cup.

'*Annabel* my favourite cup,'
'Errrrrr, it wasn't me it was the pup!'

(Well I had to blame it on someone.)

Annabel Tomlinson (11)
Brine Leas High School

THE CARETAKER

Mr Potter kept the school
Clean, neat and tidy.
But deep inside the boiler room
He kept . . .

A bag of unknown items
Which nobody knew existed
There were confiscated toys
and packets of crisps.
Chorus.

Old mobile phones
and other forms of junk
loads of smelly socks
and an even smellier skunk
Chorus.

Footballs and netballs
PE kits and footie boots
Shot puts and javelins
and even a teacher's suit?
Chorus.

Banana skins and exercise books
Pencils and pens
That old smelly bag in the boiler room
How long stuff's been in there it really depends.

Nicholas Hampson (11)
Brine Leas High School

IAN AND HIS LAZY DAD

'Ian be a dear,
and pass me a can of beer.

Ian! Oh charming son,
Go and fetch me a nice iced bun.

Ian be a good lad,
and give the tele control to your dad.

Ian! Get out of bed
I need you to get me a slice of bread.

Ian would you please,
Pass me my car keys.

Ian behave like you should,
and get me a Yorkshire pud.

Ian! Aww he's never there when you need him!'

Simon Roberts (11)
Brine Leas High School

MY FRIENDS

Fraser my friend is football mad,
Ben likes rugby and goes with his dad,
Jacob is funny and makes plenty of jokes,
And Mike is just one of the blokes.

Tommy likes Star Wars and hates yellow cars,
While Nathan likes sports and eating chocolate bars,
Stefan likes F1 and Bentleys too,
Tom Campbell never knows what he wants to do.

Matt is energetic and likes running around,
Tom likes Scalextric with realistic sound,
Markus likes texting on his mobile phone,
Ben's always downloading the latest ringtone.

Luke is Ryan's twin brother and sometimes I'm not sure,
Ryan thinks it's funny and they end up in a war.
Danny likes playing games on his PS2,
Joe likes to get anything that is cool and new.

James Dickens (12)
Brine Leas High School

SHOPPING

Shopping's a very peculiar thing
When it's for food it's a bore.
But if it's the up to date PlayStation game
Strangely enough it's no chore!

When Gramps and I go to the sweet shop
To buy lots of chocolate and mints
I stand and stare at the rows of glass jars
Till the shopkeeper drops heavy hints.

It's not so much fun when I hear my mum say,
'Please come and help me to choose.'
I know that I'm in for a long afternoon,
As I'm looking at rows of shoes!

When my stepdad says, 'Come and look on the net,
Let's find a nice villa in Spain,
One with a pool and near the sea.'
I can do that again and again.

When Mum says, 'It's school uniform that you need
Don't forget that you go back in one week.'
I get a headache, I go weak at the knees
Uniforms make me feel like a freak.

Shopping's a very peculiar thing
It's either a joy or a bore
It isn't important which place you shop in
It's really the things you shop for.

Alex Gaut (11)
Brine Leas High School

THE MOON

The moon is like a chameleon
Changing colour,
The moon is magical and mystical
It is like a disco ball
Twinkling round and round.

I'm always wondering what's up in the sky,
What is beyond the planet?
Earth, is there other living things
Other than human beings?

I always used to think the moon was made out of cheese
Getting hungry gazing at it
Why were there those holes?
Is there a mouse eating it?
I want to live on the moon.

Jacob Murphy (11)
Brine Leas High School

THE WASHING MACHINE!

The washing machine is the world
With colours of the rainbow,
Blue and green jumpers,
Are the colours of the sky and grass.
Sky and grass tumble and whirl
Tossed by the wind.
Yellow T-shirts roll around,
And form the shape of the sun.
Water fills the Earth,
Like a flood forming.
The flood settled down,
And the world carried on spinning!

Sophie Large (11)
Brine Leas High School

THE CARETAKER

There was a man, his name was Bob
and he had a cat, whose name was Scrub.
Bob worked in a school, he was a good old cleaner,
Working all day while Scrub would play!
This is the story about old Bob and his job!

Driving the car, Bob and Scrub were off to work,
It was a normal day and Scrub was looking forward
To a good old play!
All of the kids loved Scrub for his funny antics
and his weird habits!

Not far into the New Year term, Bob and Scrub were working away
When all of a sudden it was time to play!
Balls were out, the toy shed was emptied
and poor old Bob was deafened!
But all of this didn't distract him from his hard-working job!

When it was the end of the year,
Bob's retirement was coming near.
His cupboard was emptied and even Scrub had a tear in his eye
as this was the final goodbye!
After all of the years they had come to an end
and farewell messages were on the way
As everybody wished Scrub and Bob a happy departure away!

Katey Sadler (11)
Brine Leas High School

LOST IN THE AIRPORT

People rushing,
Shouting, running.
Bags being pushed.
The flight is so early.
Mother, brother, father . . . running.

They vanish down a corridor . . .

I feel so scared,
This is the end of my world.
Where are they?
Where should I go?
What must I do?

I run.
I am in a nightmare
But there is no way out.
I am doomed in a place that is unimaginable.
Still I search.
I still try to face my fears.

Nothing . . .
But a million people,
Rushing for their flights.

Sean Campbell (11)
Chesnut Lodge School

WHEN GRANDAD DIED

I remember the day,
We were in Robin Hood's bay,
The phone rang,
Mum sat on the floor,
It was Dad on the phone.
The news was sad,
Grandad had died.

I always saw him everyday.
Going to St Helen's car boot sale,
Every week.
Laughing, joking,
Watching WCW with him.
Getting Nan and Mrs Murphy,
From bingo . . . bingo . . . bingo,

I miss him.

Nathan McKie (14)
Chesnut Lodge School

LOST IN THE MOUNTAINS

Cold, windy and wet,
Walking through the mountains.
Five of us, two of them.
Running and playing, pushing and shoving.
Lee trips and slips, splashes in the water.

I see some shiny blackberries,
I stop to pick them.
I lose the group,
I feel so scared and alone.

It's cold and windy,
I walk alone.
Back to the lake
In the middle of the mountains.

Mr Roberts comes to find me,
I feel so tired.
I hear him shouting my name,
'Daniel, Daniel.'
I run up the hill. Relieved.

Daniel Reed (13)
Chesnut Lodge School

WAKING UP ILL

Waking up
The house is quiet.
The house is still.
My head aches,
My arms are sore,
Not like they felt before.
I feel sickly,
I feel prickly,
I feel alone
On my own.
No one here to say 'Hello'
Just teddy and me.
Lying in bed,
All, all alone.

Natalie Lindsay (12)
Chesnut Lodge School

MY OPERATION

I had butterflies in my tummy,
The gas made me feel funny.
The room was going darker.
Then I fell asleep.

I woke up and felt funny.
The room was spinning round and round,
Giving me butterflies in my tummy.

I looked at my leg.
It was covered in plaster
It was a funny blue.
People chattering all around,
Will they never stop?

Joshua Astill (12)
Chesnut Lodge School

LOST IN AN ARCADE IN PARIS

Music playing all around,
Games making a lot of sound.
Money dropping on the floor,
People coming through the door.

No more money,
I'll go and ask Dad.
There are a lot of pubs,
Which one is he in?
This one, that one.
He is nowhere
To be seen.
My arms feel numb.
I start to run.
A tear rolls down my face,
My heart began to race.

Where is my dad?
I feel very sad.
Will I ever see him again?
I have a very bad pain.
People laughing and going mad,
Am I the only one who is sad?

A man is running very fast . . .
Yes, yes . . . it's my dad.

Jane Parker (13)
Chesnut Lodge School

LIKE AN OBSESSION

My cousin Dale, like a possession
Like an obsession.
I'm *OK,* I'm saved thanks to Dale.
Like an obsession, like a possession.

His face, his eyes, gone.
He said goodbye.
I did not know why.
He left us all.

I was going to fall,
He was my only protection.
He was not only my cousin.
He was my best friend.

Dale like a possession,
Like an obsession.

Chelsea Norton (12)
Chesnut Lodge School

HELP!

It gives them pleasure to see me break,
In the centre of a circle of hate!
No friends
No hope
No life
They don't know what it's like
Why?
Because I'm black
The one small difference between me and them . . .
Why?
Why do they make my life like this?

Stewart Cain (14)
Hartford High School

MY LOVEABLE GRANDAD

My grandad he was a wonderful man
He brought our family closer,
Every part of him had a tan
and he once found a four-leaf clover.

His hair was as shiny as gold
Everything he did was thoughtful in every way,
He was there when we were cold
Sometimes he did whatever we'd say.

His hands were soft as pillows
and his heart was pure as can be,
Me and my sisters were his little fellows
I always sat on his knee.

He took us on long walks
It was like they would never end,
and throughout the day he talks
Along all the windy bends.

He loved having barbecues
Bringing all his friends round,
Some of them travelled a lot with him
and time to time went to Dover.

He was like a happy helper in the house
Doing everything from tip to toe,
He once hid from a mouse
and could never tie his bows.

I remember him as well as I can
From when I was born to the last day,
I remember all his cups and pans
and mostly everything he did say.

Lisa Yould (12)
Hartford High School

PREJUDICES

Just shut up!
I don't care about your hung-up judgements.
Keep them to yourself.
Sure, you're entitled to your beliefs,
I just prefer mine.

You hate her 'cause she's a different colour.
You call everyone who annoys you 'Gay'.
Not in a derogatory way of course.
Do you ever think before you speak?
Open your mouth to reveal your closed mind.

Do you believe what you hear on the news?
No doubt you do.
So much death. Everyday.
Prejudices - a gun to someone's head.

Don't say your hatred doesn't run that deep,
You don't have to.
It's in your blood, the anger that you were subjected to everyday.
Don't like them, they're different.
Don't listen to 'them' they're *different.*
Who's the 'them'?
What does that make 'us'?
Don't question your beliefs.

My beliefs make me who I am.
Who are you?

Claire Bagnall (15)
Hartford High School

FOOTBALL CRAZY

We all walked in
It was about to begin
Everyone cheered and waved
While the players played
It was raining very hard.

My dad made a bet
When it got very wet
He said that Goater would score
When it began to pour.

The sun dried the rain,
When the player felt pain
There was a big injury
And a red card
The opposition thought it was getting hard.

My dad started to cheer
Because Goater had scored
He had won the bet
And a ten pound he would get.

The game had finished
Man City had won.
Poor Stockport were crying.
When we went home
We queued in a line for a while.
The game was over.

David Wood (12)
Hartford High School

My Nanna

The first memory of my nanna
Her little grey car
It chugged along the road,
Windows down, music loud,
She always liked a bit of fun.
As she grew old time overtook her.
She slowed down and gradually fell ill.
All because of those white sticks of death.
Her car went and the doors closed,
She never left her seat.
The hospital was our second home,
We knew all the nurses by first name,
The dog slowed down too,
The house seemed dull,
She sat all day lonely,
Still full of life, but the sparkle had gone.
I remember one day I bought some trousers,
She wanted the same fashionable pair.
She didn't take them off.
Now she has gone, I feel empty,
A piece of the puzzle was gone
What am I to do?

Katie Garner (15)
Hartford High School

SPORTS DAY

We sit in rows
The nerves increase
Waiting for my lonely race.

My name is called
I slowly walk
To my starting place.

The gun is fired
I jump in shock
Then sprint to catch that person in front.

I'm halfway there
and wondering why
I ever chose
to take that place.

The line draws near
I edge in front
Then *zoom*
there goes the opposing force.

Fifths not bad
I hear them say
if only six had took their place.

Laura Fuller (15)
Hartford High School

SOMEONE'S AT THE DOOR

Rat-a-tap tap
Someone's at the door
Clankety clank
Down the corridor
The old wooden door is unbolted
Who is it?
Nobody knows.

> A woman from the streets
> Neglected
> Rejected
> Alone in the middle of London
> Giving birth to a baby boy.

The rain patters on the windowpane
Crashes of lightning
Booms of thunder
The mysterious woman takes one last breath
Looks at her child
And falls to death.

Sophie Scott (12)
Hartford High School

OLIVER'S POEM

O   ther people, happy sighs
L   ittle boys live or die
I   n the streets and on the road
V   ery cold and all alone
E   verywhere food I see
R   eally happy, won't you feed me?

Lucy Washburn (12)
Hartford High School

GRANDAD FRED

I remember my grandad
From times long gone by,
From times when he smiled,
And his moustache smiled 'Hi.'
From times in the garden,
And times by the sea,
I remember my grandad
He made me happy.

I remember my grandad,
From times later on,
When he lived in a hospice,
And was sealed from
All life except ours,
And his that was gone,
And my grandma who really did try
To just carry on.

Living and loving,
And crying too,
All for my grandad
His life almost through.

Zack Adlington (13)
Hartford High School

OLIVER

O   ne lonely child
L   onging for a family
I   n one enormous world
V   iolent carers
E   very chance he jumps for freedom
R   elying on strangers to keep him safe.

Emily Godden (11)
Hartford High School

OLIVER TWIST

O nce upon a time,
L ived a young boy called Oliver
I n a very, very lonely life
V ery cautious of all his actions
E very scrap of food is precious
R eading and writing are a mystery to Oliver.

T he boy has no family to come and save him from his lonely life.
W andering the streets trying to find somebody to take him in.
I n trouble, is Oliver's life story
S earching for food to eat and water to drink
T ime will tell if he will survive.

Frances Clarke (12)
Hartford High School

OLIVER TWIST

O liver had a hard life
L eft at the workhouse from birth
I n Mr Sowerberry's house,
V ery scared
E very creak and rattle haunting him
R eading the plaques on coffins.

T he run-ins with the law,
W hen he was Fagin's lad.
I n a cell when wrongly accused.
S till he's safe now,
T he long lost grandfather rescuing him.

Sarah Reilly (12)
Hartford High School

OLIVER!

O nly scraps of food to eat
L iving on the street
I n a very lonely life
V ery very unhappy
E ternal misery
R ivers of tears stream down his face.

T he boy all alone with no one to talk to
W ith no family or friends
I n trouble with the law constantly
S adly wandering the streets
T he clothes on his back, all he owns.

Chloe Carter (12)
Hartford High School

OLIVER TWIST

O rphaned from birth
L onely with no one to lean on
I nfluenced by mischievous boys
V agrants take him in
E very move is crucial
R etreating quickly

T ime is of the essence
W anting to escape this life
I nnocent until proven guilty
S aved by a long lost grandfather
T ragedy is no more.

Amy Sumner (12)
Hartford High School

OI REF!

Oi ref!
The rain poured down,
As the crowd took a deep breath.
The defender has scored,
The ref ran to the player and issued a no goal.
Oi ref!

Oi ref!
As half-time drew closer,
Manchester United had a penalty
The supporters were anxious
He kicked the ball and scored
The crowd erupted with cheers and boos
Oi ref!

Oi ref!
As the whistle blew,
Manchester 1 Vics 0.
With heads drooped low,
We made our way to the gates,
Our clothes were soaking
Oi ref!

Amy Winnington (12)
Hartford High School

DODGER

D   odging the law
O   n his way to Australia
D   odger stealing his way to the top
G   reat friend
E   ager to steal
R   unning from the law.

Tom Whitehurst (11)
Hartford High School

THE BEACH!

The beach was great
Jellyfish made us run
We played footie on the warm sand
The sea was as cold as ice.

We ate ice cream
Candyfloss made our fingers sticky
We went crab hunting
Then let them go afterwards.

The sun was hot
Seagulls stole our food
The waves crashed against the rocks
Empty bottles drifted through the sand
Shells broke from under our feet
People knocked over our sandcastles
People gave us dirty looks
As we were on our blown-up dolphin.

Kelly-Marie Towers (13)
Hartford High School

BILL SYKES

B   ad boy of Fagin's gang
      the worst in the town
I   think he is evil and he
      deserves to be in jail
L   iar of the group in the
      pub selling illegal goods
L   outish killer of Nancy,
      his so called lawful wife.

Tom Blain (11)
Hartford High School

STARS

Stars,
  sparkle in the night sky
Stars,
  twinkle in the darkness
Stars,
  never have to worry
Stars,
  have no parents to tell them off
Stars,
  have no untidy rooms to clean
Stars,
  Oh I wish I was one.

Kirsty Sayle (13)
Hartford High School

ARTFUL DODGER

A wfully cunning
R oams around London
T o look for his prey
F ulfilling his task to pick-pocket
U ntil the day is over and the
L ights start to dim.

D on't try and stop him
O n every chance he gets
D odger will take
G uarantee he will be there
E very time you have a
R emote amount of money.

Zoe Lucock (11)
Hartford High School

ON A DESERT ISLAND

As I sat there on the sand,
The water slowly washing over my feet,
I looked out across the sea, and could just make out
A vague outline of crowds of people on land,
I thought to myself how nice and peaceful it was here
on this island by myself.

As I sat there on the sand,
The only noise that could be heard was the seagulls
Flying up above and the water hitting the golden shore.

As I sat there on the sand,
Mesmerised by the sparkling waves,
I picked up a handful of sand and slowly let it fall back down.
I sat there watching the sun go down.
As the sky turned pink I decided it was time to go
But as I went, I was sad to leave.

Georgia Bramhall (12)
Hartford High School

OLIVER'S CHANT

(Sung to a military chant tune)

Bill Sykes and Fagin's Gang,
Fagin's den is where they hang
Dodger, Charlie, Fagin too,
They've all got a crime to do.
Robbing, stealing, nicking dosh,
Trying to make it so they're posh.
That's about it for Fagin's Gang,
'Cept for the part where they all get hanged.

Johanna Lawrence (12)
Hartford High School

WHERE IS SHE?

Where is she? Where is she?
It's 8pm
Was it 8.15 or not?
Where is she? Where is she?
I am really worried
I love her dearly.
Where is she? Where is she?
The time's half eight
I think I am going to faint.
Where is she? Where is she?
Her room's not tidy
She lied to me.
Where is she? Where is she?
It's 9pm
She should have been here on the dot.
Where is she? Where is she?
It's 10pm
She's home
I was so worried
I am going to bed.

Hannah Crompton (12)
Hartford High School

OLIVER

O   ver the streets of London Oliver roams
L   onely and begging for food
I   n his heart there is fear and anger
V   ery little food to live on
E   veryone passes without a blink
R   eally needing his family by his side.

Zoe Lawrence (12)
Hartford High School

OLIVER TWIST

O liver in the horrible workhouse
L ike a flea against a dragon
I   t - flicking it away
V icious to his victim
E ating wasn't possible
R egretting he met this fate

I   n the dreaded workhouse
N eeding a family

T ension building up
H aunting him since birth
E vil to the young boy (Oliver)

W orking for nothing
O utside of this monster is a world of beauty
R esisting against fate
K idnapped by the cruel world
H oping life will get better
O ptimistic he was
U nsuccessful
S oon he will get out of here
E ver waiting.

Ashleigh Hopps (12)
Hartford High School

THE BEACH

The blazing sun shines in my face as I paddle my feet.
Children playing, men fishing.
Music blasting, seagulls screeching.
Mums sunbathing, while Dads drink beer.
The pier is full, every direction I look I see people.

Andrew Finemore (13)
Hartford High School

THE SHOW

The clock is ticking as dancers arrive
Costume bags and make-up in their hands
All the dancers pile into the school gym
One hour to the show!

Hair and make-up being done
Year 7s running around like loonies
Will they ever calm down?
Forty minutes to the show!

Costumes being put on
The audience start to arrive!
Nerves start to pile up!
Twenty minutes to the show!

The first half dancers wait by the hall door
The head teacher gives a quick speech
I'm on first and my nerves start to rise!
Ten minutes to the show!

The head takes a seat
The lights dim down
I can't do this!
Two minutes to the show!

I walk on stage to take my position
Fifteen others follow and do the same
The lights come on followed by the music
The show starts!

My nerves disappear!
I'm enjoying this!
The lights and music go down!
I come off the stage!

Quick! Get changed!
The next dance starts in five minutes!
My adrenaline has hit the roof!
I hope the show never ends!

Siobhan Eyes (15)
Hartford High School

TURNED TO STONE!

I may be stone but my heart still beats,
I lie around the water so deep.

I cannot see or hear,
But I can sense she's still near.

She's the monster you have to ignore,
If you don't you will be lying with me on the floor.

I shout out in my mind but no one can hear,
The words I need to say do not appear.

All I can do is wait and wait,
To find out what is my fate.

Many come many fail
To kill this monster is only a fairy tale.

But wait what is this,
A knight that did not miss?

The monster is killed, she is dead,
Now I can rest my weary head.

Once again I feel the breeze,
As the water splashes at my knees.

Sarah Dutton (13)
Hartford High School

THE SEASIDE

I step onto the soft, golden sand.
The glistening sun, beaming onto my little yellow
sunhat.
I walk down towards the shimmering sea,
Past the colourful shells and rocks.
The sea crashing down onto my tiny cold feet.
Yachts up ahead sailing gracefully along the horizon.
Rockpools to the left, full of slimy, green seaweed.
The ice cream van travels along the sandy beach.
My ice cream is melting with strawberry sauce.
I grab my bucket and spade,
Then I make a huge sandcastle, details and all.
The sun's going down, down to the horizon.
The seaside is empty all but me,
The sea will always be there,
With the golden soft sand and beaming sun.
With the crashing waves and rock pools.
The seaside will always be there.

Claire Jones (12)
Hartford High School

A DEMONSTRATION

The sky was as grey as cold metal.
The wind howled as a captured cat does, tearing against its leash.
The protesters stood against injustice as trees stand against wind and
rain.
Their banners were like bees, stinging the objects of their anger.
The gate was like a bully, stopping people doing the right thing.
The building was like a giant, standing whatever those around it
might do.

Maria Higson (13)
Hartford High School

KATIE DAVIES

Her hair in tiny curls of gold,
Her eyes like the deep blue sea.
Teeth growing like little pegs,
And hands as small as little waving starfish.
Her soft feet pattering on the floor,
Nails as tiny as grains of sand.
Her whole body only the size of my arm.

Her scream as piercing it will break eardrums,
Her laugh so high it will touch the sky.
Her clothes as cute as a little puppy's fur,
She had chickenpox I remember the day well.
    Her name is Katie Davies.

Amy Holehouse (12)
Hartford High School

SUMMER HOLIDAYS

S   ummer holidays here, as I climb out of bed
U   nforgettable burning heat, pounds my head
M   any children play around on the beach
M   y family holiday, sane friends out of reach
E   ach day is different from the one before
R   eading and sunbathing: 'Such a chore!'

H   ome is such a distance away
O   n holidays better, I want to stay!
L   ong flight home, home to sleep
S   chool is back . . . *next week!*

Lisa Noden (15)
Hartford High School

THROUGH THAT DOOR

Through that door
Is a world of chocolate,
Chocolate roads and chocolate cars,
Houses made of chocolate bars,
Chocolate trees and chocolate flowers,
We can eat for hours and hours,
Chocolate chickens lay chocolate eggs,
Horses run with chocolate legs,
Chocolate fish in a chocolate lake,
Now I've got a tummy ache.

Through that door
Is a fantasy island,
Coconut trees and bright blue sea,
Monkeys carrying cups of tea,
Penguins sitting in the sun,
Everyone having lots of fun,
No homework and no cauliflower,
Watching TV any hour.

Through that door,
Is a shopping fantasy,
Fashion shops and jewellery too,
Dresses and tops all for you,
Lots of colour
Lots of choice
Take big bags because,
It's all free.

Through that door
Is a fairground,
Candyfloss and hot dogs too,
Whizzy rides just for you.

Up and down we bounce around,
In the sky and down to ground.
Noisy music, flashing lights
Fireworks brighten up the night.

Sophie Landreth (11)
Hartford High School

FIRST WRESTLING EVENT!

Screaming fans
Anticipation across the stands
Sweat boiling down your face
But none of the energy gone to waste
Then the fireworks hit.

The smell of burning metal
Then the smell began to settle
The music hits, the lights flash
The fans got louder and louder
Until the stands began to shake
Then the fireworks came awake.

They all come out to play
Now it was their opponents time to pray
The thump of their bodies as they hit the ground
The pound of the weapon as it hits their face
Now it's their time to say grace.

1, 2, 3
It was the end of the match
Now it's the time to detach
The loser walks away in shame
The winner walks away with fame.

Tom Mercer (12)
Hartford High School

FIRST PLANE RIDE

The sweet smell of the delicious food
Coming around the aeroplane.

        The scenery of all the miniature houses
        And cars below.

People relaxing,
Talking, reading,
Just enjoying the ride.

        I feel so excited
        Yet I am nervous about the flight.

People listening to music,
The radio and good tapes.

        Fastening our seatbelts getting ready
        For landing, our holiday has nearly started.

Emily Lindsay (12)
Hartford High School

THINGS I LOVE

I love my stuffed dog as I squeeze it.
I love the humour of the Simpsons.
I love the addictive smell of petrol.
I love the softness of my pet cats.
I love sourness of lemons.
I love watching the Arsenal games when Thierry Henry scores.
I love the taste of salt and vinegar crisps as it slides down my throat.
I love the liqueur of WKD as it drips down my throat.
I love the radio as it brings music to my ears.
I love the beach as I surf in the warm sea.

Martin Cadman (12)
Hartford High School

AUSTRALIA

I want to go to Australia,
I want to visit the whole island.
For my friends I will bring back lots of parafinalia,
I want to go to Australia because England is bland,
I want to go to the rainforest,
I want a guided tour,
The Australian wildlife is more poisonous than the rest,
I will have to buy anti venom from the store.
I want to go to the Great Barrier Reef,
I want to go snorkelling,
I want to stay there a long time not to make my visit brief,
The Aborigines I will visit with witch doctors cackling.
I want to visit Ayers Rock
And climb up the side,
I want to go to Sydney dock,
I want to go to the opera; something I've never tried.
I don't like flying though,
It's cramped, uncomfortable and makes me sick.
Although I do like being in the air like a crow.
I'm not scared of flying, so don't take the mick.

Ed Hunt (14)
Hartford High School

A GIRL IN MY CLASS

If she was a piece of furniture she'd be a grandfather clock,
tall and slim but sometimes foreboding!
As a fruit she would be an orange: sweet but having many sections.
Her sound is a trumpet, making her views very clear.
She's red, always very determined,
if she was a country she'd be Panama, small but very significant.

Rachel Ward (13)
Hartford High School

My Grandma

My grandma is always happy like a sunny day
She comes to meet me from school with the dog.
When I go to her house it smells fresh and clean,
My grandma is kind and never mean.

My grandma makes me laugh, she's like the joker in a pack of cards.
I love to go on long walks with her,
We have so much fun.

She wears glasses and has nice blond hair
Whatever she has she always shares.
At night I make her a drink in her special mug,
Then she says goodnight and gives me a big hug!

Rachael Wilson (13)
Hartford High School

Grandad

G enerous is my grandad all the time
R ussell is his name the same as my dad
A ddicted to smoking, but always has humour
N othing can stop him from achieving his goal
   even if it is a mountain
D ozens of jokes he cracks each day
   this is his way
A fter tea he likes to go fishing.
   It is his favourite thing
D elightfully helpful he is to us all,
   he gives me money then I spend it straight away.

Aaron Whalley (12)
Hartford High School

THE BEACH

I run onto the beach
The hot sand burning under my feet
The sun searing my back
All around children playing
Digging holes and building sandcastles
The ice cream man calling 'Get your ice cream!'
Children gathering around
Waves increasing making a bath of foam
Sand dunes as big as mountains
Seagulls squawk
Kites soaring through the sky
Yachts sailing through the sea
Now it is time to leave the beach
Sun sinks behind the dunes
The beach is now deserted.

Mark Parker (12)
Hartford High School

ISSY

Her eyes are as blue as the sea on a sunny afternoon.
Her hair is as blonde as the sand on a tropical beach.
Her skin is the colour of a peach.
She is seven and I think she is an angel from Heaven.

Her singing is just like birds early in the morning.
She is always listening to Avril Lavigne
and she thinks that she is her sister.
Issy is as cuddly as a newborn puppy.

Steven Moore (12)
Hartford High School

HOW COME I'M DESERTED?

Picked up by the tail and ear.
No food in my bowl to eat.
Wanting to be found by somebody caring
How come I'm deserted?

Wishing I could be loved, huddled and fed
Crying and squealing at the top of my voice
Always wished I could be washed by my mum
How come I'm deserted?

Home alone in this hell of a dump
Children throwing sticks and stones at me
Darkness is the place for me
How come I'm deserted?

Emily Birch (14)
Hartford High School

BLUE PLANET

B   eautiful water shimmers and shines as fish swim around
L   ittle fish, big sharks, they all live in the same world
U   nder the viewing tube I watch the games the fish play
E   very fish has a different life, colour, fin.

P   eople watch and, wonder how they came to be
L   ovely coral to make the fish feel at home
A   ll of the fish chase one another around the enormous tanks
N   one of the sharks will eat the fish, they get their own food from us
E   very time a person walks past the aquatic creatures scatter
T   hrough the glass I watch them twirl and twiz,
    leaving a mist of shiny bubbles.

Becky Walsh (12)
Hartford High School

THE POINT OF NO RETURN

The borders have been crossed
The point of no return
The order has been given
The troops must go in
The point of no return.

The line has been crossed
The point of no return.

Innocent lives ruined
Friendly line, how friendly?
Irreparable damage
No remorse.

The line has been crossed
The point of no return.

Sam Greenwood (16)
Hartford High School

HONEY

Soft, cute and funny
My floppy-eared bunny
Her name is Honey.

She is so sweet
I give her a treat
So she runs over with her pounding feet.

I put her back in her cage
She rolls over like a page
Then runs round inspite of rage.

April Conway (14)
Hartford High School

I Should Like To Rise And Go . . .

I should like to rise and go,
To mountains high and valleys low.
To beaches filled with golden sand,
Or paradise in a deserted land.

I would go where trees grow tall,
And watch colourful leaves begin to fall.
I would walk for hours and hours,
To look at exotic plants and flowers.

I'd listen to the gentle sounds of the sea,
And watch the sun set in front of me.
And when the sun's gone and it starts to feel cold,
I'd leave and walk in fields of gold.

And if on my travels I start to feel alone,
I could always turn back,
And go straight home.
But if ever again
I begin to feel bored,
I'd catch a plane and fly abroad.

Katie Richardson (14)
Hartford High School

Bird

B   eautiful and graceful
I   mmaculate in looks
R   iding like thermals gracefully
D   iving fast to capture its prey.

Gareth Smith (13)
Hartford High School

THE MOON AND THE STARS

This sky is dark
The moon is bright
Let's see if it shines tonight
It shines in the moonlight sky
With the stars glistening among it
Placing light around the world
The moon and the stars play an important role
They all have self control
So next time you are in your house
Do not go and fuss the mouse
Just look at the moon and stars
And admire the light
On this wonderful
   Glistening night.

Laura Stafford (12)
Hartford High School

MY CAT

My cat is amazing
He can play the guitar
He may not be an actor
But he's a pussy superstar.

My cat is everywhere
We watch him on TV
He may not be an actor
But he's a pussy superstar.

He can eat a whole watermelon
 My cat
 My cat.

Rachael Deakin (14)
Hartford High School

THE LAST DOG

I am the last dog
the forgotten dog
an old toy,
I haven't got a name
but who would claim
this last, forgotten dog?
I am the last dog
the forgotten dog,
an old toy,
but why am I the last dog?
I haven't done anything wrong,
I am the last dog,
the forgotten dog,
an old toy.
If I was a pedigree,
would you play with me?

Emma Sherwood (13)
Hartford High School

I SHOULD LIKE TO RISE AND GO

I should like to rise and go,
Where beaches lie as white as snow,
And the sea shines a turquoise blue,
I'd love to go, wouldn't you?

The palm trees rustle in the breeze,
And the way of life - laid back at ease . . .
Where people dance on the moonlit sands,
Come just take me by the hand.

Emily Pargeter (14)
Hartford High School

WHY IS IT ALWAYS ME?

Bang the sound of the cane hitting my skull
Trying to hide into a ball, like it's all unreal.
My fur changing, falling out with fright,
Why? Why is it always me?

Running behind the sofa, when the owners return.
Wishing I could be strong and hard like a block of ice.
Screaming sounds, vibrating through my head,
Why? Why is it always me?

Am I really that sad, boring and pathetic,
It's not my fault I'm only a cat, and can't do much.
I really wish, I was the cat from next door,
He's well looked after, fed and loved. So . . .
Why? Why is it always me?

Emma Beech (14)
Hartford High School

I'LL WAIT

When I first came, you loved me and fed me,
you walked me and calmed me.

But now you bash me and trash me,
and you starve me and kick me,
but I wait for the owners I used to know.

You hurt me and beat me,
you throw me and smack me,
but I still wait for the owner I used to know.

Now you stab me and jab me,
you laugh as I weep but now I can't wait any more . . .
I am happy now.

Gareth Davies (14)
Hartford High School

TO RISE AND GO

I should like to rise and go
To see the sand and then the snow.
To watch the sun set on the rock
To swim by the reef and feel life stop.

I should like to go and see
What the outback holds for me.
To go and see a friend of mine,
And then, together pass the time.

I should like to see and touch
If just to say, 'I thought as much!'
I'd like to feel the coral reef
And check Ayres Rock is really steep.

I'd like to touch and breathe the air,
In the outback's piercing stare.
To feel the hotness of the sun,
And with the wildlife start to run.

Rachel Bury (14)
Hartford High School

MY BROTHER

S   tuart Yardley is seventeen
T   hough he acts thirteen.
U   gly Stuart with brown hair
A   nd calls his sister a little mare.
R   ubbing cream on his tattoo.
T   he stupid boy scares me when he says,
            'Boo!'

Ben Yardley (12)
Hartford High School

THE WHALES

As the sun raises over the Atlantic Ocean,
The whales wake to the early sun.
Their glittering eyes raise to the sun;
For it's time to eat.
Young 'uns cry for their mothers
As fathers catch their dinner.

The whales chat
In a silent, secret language,
Which I will never know.
The sky turns pink
And the whales know
It's time to rest
For the day ahead.

Gooleswari Seeburn (12)
Hartford High School

POEMS ABOUT PEOPLE

My brother Mike sums up his life on his computer,
Hours upon hours, typing away, tapping on the keyboard,
Like a woodpecker pecking on the window.

He sits in his chair,
Chatting away to the people in the chatroom,
He says he will be out of his room soon.

He comes down for his tea,
He is now with his best friend Lee.

He sits in his room with his mates,
Talking to someone he really hates.

Catherine Riley (12)
Hartford High School

THE MAZE

The maze is full of shining eyes.
The maze is full of creeping feet.
The maze is full of tiny cries.
You must not go into the maze tonight.

Walking through the misty haze
I seem to be in a tricky maze.
Scared and cold I walk around
And find a stranger on the ground.

The maze is full of shiny eyes.
The maze is full of creeping feet.
The maze is full of tiny cries.
You must not go into the maze tonight.

The man woke up and gave me a fright.
On that cold and scary, eerie night.
His skin was pale and cold as ice.
But his character was very nice.

The maze is full of shiny eyes.
The maze is full of creeping feet.
The maze is full of tiny cries.
You must not go into the maze tonight.

His fingers were curly.
His nose was bent.
His eyes were bloodshot
And his mouth was rent.

The maze is full of shining eyes.
The maze is full of creeping feet.
The maze is full of tiny cries.
You must not go into the maze tonight.

He showed me the way from this scary place.
Which means you can't judge someone by their face.
We shook hands and said goodbye.
When I turned my back, I began to cry.

The maze is full of shining eyes.
The maze is full of creeping feet.
The maze is full of tiny cries.
You must not go into the maze tonight.

Daniel Ward (12)
Hartford High School

I WOULD LIKE TO RISE AND GO!

I would like to rise and go
To leave my daily life
The chores and work would be behind
Off I'd go without a thought in mind.

To the Bahamas sandy beaches
To watch the palm tree as it slowly reaches
Towards the waves on the moonlit beaches
I'd soak up the rays
Whilst watching fishermen working in the bays.

Or go on skis down a mountain side
Lightly and gracefully would I glide
Or else sit side by side on a dog sleigh ride
To watch a child stand and cry
Because she didn't get to try.

I would like to rise and go!

Laura Lambert (15)
Hartford High School

THE OCEAN

The ocean is full of glistening eyes
The ocean is full of tiny fish
The ocean is full of shining bubbles
You must not go into the ocean at night.

I met a shark with glaring teeth
His eyes were like shining diamonds
A body so strong and tail so swift
As fast it's prey no place to hide.

The ocean is full of glistening eyes
The ocean is full of tiny fish
The ocean is full of shining bubbles
You must not go into the ocean at night.

The silent hunter patrolled the deep
Searching all day and night for something to eat.

The ocean is full of glistening eyes
The ocean is full of tiny fish
The ocean is full of shining bubbles
You must not go into the ocean at night.

If you see me swimming nearby please don't stop to say, 'hi'
Hungry is my second name and will eat anybody just the same.

The ocean is full of glistening eyes
The ocean is full of tiny fish
The ocean is full of shining bubbles
You must not go into the ocean at night.

Carly Beeson (12)
Hartford High School

MAGIC PLACES

The jungle is full of shining leaves
The jungle is full of creeping trees
The jungle is full of slimy slugs
You must not go in the jungle at night.

I met a gorilla with eyes of scales
And a foot of hairy tails
And fur all pink with crawling bugs
And a hand of slimy slugs.

The jungle is full of shining leaves
The jungle is full of creeping trees
The jungle is full of slimy slugs
You must not go in the jungle at night.

He told me a poem back to front
And he gave me the biggest grunt
I saw eyes at the back of his head
And he told me his name was Ted.

The jungle is full of shining leaves
The jungle is full of creeping trees
The jungle is full of slimy slugs
You must not go in the jungle at night.

He told me he was very lost
And he will have to pay a big cost
He was meant to get the snake that ran away
But he found he had tooth decay.

Nicola Steen (12)
Hartford High School

THROUGH THAT DOOR

Through that door
Is a big screen for films
The flashing lights
The screen full of bloody fights
Where you watch what you want
Food for you
Cushioned seats too.

Through that door is space
Where you can float around
Nowhere near the ground
This is space
My favourite place.

Through that door is a volcano
Hot boiling lava
The sights are great
But if you are not careful
This might be your fate.

Through that door is the cyclops
With his giant body
And his big eye
But be careful
He is sly.

Leigh Madeley (12)
Hartford High School

THROUGH THAT DOOR

Through that door is
A Caribbean beach.
White sand,
The sea is peach.

Through that door is
A theme park,
High rides,
Small rides,
Arcades,
Pick 'n' mix.

Through that door is
A Ferrari shop!
A silver Ferrari Spider
200mph
With leather seats!

Through that door is
Rome in Italy,
With Italia and Calvin Klein,
And to think, it's all mine.

Through that door is
A football pitch -
The grass like a carpet,
With Dejan Stankovitche
It's my new back garden.

Michael Rathbone (12)
Hartford High School

POEMS ABOUT PLACES

The ocean is full of glistening waters,
The ocean is full of colourful creatures,
The ocean is full of animal laughter,
It is a wonderful place to be at night.

A grey, magnificent creature lifts up from the water,
An intelligent animal it seems,
It jumps through the water as happy as can be,
And it chatters to his friend as it swims.

The ocean is full of glistening waters,
The ocean is full of colourful creatures,
The ocean is full of animal laughter,
It is a wonderful place to be at night.

Its face so sweet so kind and innocent,
It was like a best friend to me,
I had never seen a creature so talented before,
The reflection of his face was reflected on the water.

The ocean is full of glistening waters,
The ocean is full of colourful creatures,
The ocean is full of animal laughter,
It is a wonderful place to be at night.

As the sun starts to rise, I head back to shore,
The mammal leapt through the water following the boat,
Then it realizes I am leaving and its shiny blue eyes fall sad,
He turns reluctantly back to its family to its territory.

The ocean is full of glistening waters,
The ocean is full of colourful creatures,
The ocean is full of animal laughter
It is a wonderful place to be at night.

Sarah Thompson (12)
Hartford High School

THE HAUNTED HOUSE

The house is full of shining lights
The house is full of eerie sounds
The house is full of tiny bugs
You must not enter the house at night.

I went to the house to use the phone
Then I heard a very loud groan
I checked it out and there was a ghost
With big eyes and a massive cloak.

The house is full of shining lights
The house is full of eerie sounds
The house is full of tiny bugs
You must not enter the house at night.

The ghost told me to follow
I could hardly swallow
I tried to get away
But he threatened me to stay.

The house is full of shining lights
The house is full of eerie sounds
The house is full of tiny bugs
You must not enter the house at night.

The ghost grabbed me by my neck
Then he threw me on the deck
I tried to get away but he said '*Na*'
But I luckily got to run away.

The house is full of shining lights
The house is full of eerie sounds
The house is full of tiny bugs
You must not enter the house at night.

Craig Douglas (12)
Hartford High School

A BROKEN HOUSEHOLD

Yesterday, all was silent,
No shouting but no talking,
The atmosphere of a silent movie,
Today Mum's crying and Dad's shouting.
I don't know what to do,
It feels like life's all a dream,
My head full of fears.
Everyone's uptight and angry,
All I can do is cry.

Yesterday, Dad walked out,
Why did he get involved with that other woman?
All Mum could do was cry.
Today, all is loud because Dad is back.
He went on the bottle last night,
He's like a schizophrenic monster.
Dad's shouting, Mum's crying,
Sisters screaming like a kettle squealing.
All I want to do is die.

Tomorrow will be different,
I won't be here,
It's all too much for my head to take,
It's going to explode.
Nothing ever goes right now,
Not like it used to,
There's a knife in the kitchen,
But no, I will always look up,
I will use positive thinking,
Tomorrow will be a *better* day!

Fiona Washington (14)
Hartford High School

MAZE

The maze is tricky and turning
The maze is long and winding
The maze is lost and gloomy
Even in light, the maze is a fright!

I met some giant spiders,
Some were right behind us.
We've turned all the corners,
Now night has fallen before us!

The maze is tricky and turning
The maze is long and winding
The maze is lost and gloomy
Even in light, the maze is a fright!

A man who followed us round,
Knew we were lost not found,
He told us now we're here
The maze is full of fear!

The maze is tricky and turning
The maze is long and winding
The maze is lost and gloomy
Even in light, the maze is a fright!

The maze just started whirling,
Our heads kept on turning
They I smelt some burning
My stomach was churning!

The maze is tricky and turning
The maze is long and winding
The maze is lost and gloomy
Even in light, the maze is a fright!

Rebecca Johnson (11)
Hartford High School

ALL THINGS THAT MATTER TO ME

My fat dog barks like a frog and nuzzles my arms and face.
His name is Zac, he didn't come in a pack, we picked him up instead.

My cousin's cat Britney, could have bit me, but licked my
                                                    arm instead,
Small and cute, soft and sweet, snuggled up in her nice warm bed.

Chocolate melting in my mouth, sweet, delicious, silky-brown and tasty
With caramel, great for nibbling and also very milky.

Fresh summer breeze, cool like frozen peas
Blowing my hair and face.

My whole family, brother doing stuff he shouldn't be we will always
                                                    be the same,
Even if my brother Declan drives us all insane

Underwater scenes, cool, calm, blue, colder than cold,
Deeper than deep enough to give you the flu.

Jade Prior (11)
Hartford High School

DOLPHINS!

The dolphin wears a grey leather jacket.
As grey as the clouds when raining.
It jumps through the sea.
It jumps and somersaults so elegantly.
When they talk they squeak.
Dolphins have always been my favourite animals
And I hope that they shall live till the end of my time.

Bryher Shirley (12)
Hartford High School

I WOULD LIKE TO RISE AND GO

I would like to rise and go,
A place where only I would only know,
Underneath a starry night,
With only a small light in sight.
Dreaming of where I can go,
In the place where I would only know.

After I had been there,
I sit under a tree eating a delicious pear,
Then I stroll over the beach,
Hoping that the dream I want I can reach.
Underneath the glittering sun,
Playing with shells all day, having fun.

Then I wake up in a sudden shock,
Realising I slept on a dirty old rock,
I lay there knowing where I could go,
Somewhere I go when I'm feeling low,
So when I want to rise and go,
I'll go to the place only I shall know.

Katie Searby (15)
Hartford High School

A POEM OF CREATURES

My pet ants, they're so cool, they are absolutely minuscule,
The shark lies in the dark at the bottom of the muddy, murky seabed,
There is a bird that lives at the bottom of my garden,
It flies from tree to tree and does a somersault in the gentle breeze.
My cat Zipy is as quick as a bee
And as I shout, 'Zipy, it is teatime,'
She is here with a flick of the wrist.

James Pickup (11)
Hartford High School

GLADIATOR

I was once a lame slave,
When my wife was put in her grave,
And my son went with her,
Company he would give her.

I was sold to one of many schools,
Where we were forced to use lethal tools,
Swords, armour, axes, you name it,
Skilled warriors wore the whole kit.

I had never been so scared in my life,
When I was handed a net, a shield and a knife,
I was told to enter the spectacle,
And if I killed, I would be respectable.

Big strong men waved swords as I went in,
Then the master shouted, 'Begin!'
I took a hefty blow in the side,
All my anger, I could no longer hide.

I went in search of the man who had struck me,
I parried more blows until I could see,
He was lying on his chest with his face in the sand,
Not far from him lay his weapon and his hand.

Even now he's dead, I must not forget,
That this bloodied battle is not over yet.
Everywhere on the arena floor,
Men had been slain, my eyes before.

Many enemies were still alive,
From my sweeping sword, they'd duck and dive,
But like all the others, they would fall,
Until the master made the final call.

The master summoned me to stand on a board,
Then he gave me a wooden sword,
'Now I'm free,' I said to myself,
That's another trophy to add to my shelf.

Lewis Price-Milne (13)
Hartford High School

GRANDAD

I remember my grandad as a happy man,
Always cracking jokes that weren't funny
Singing his favourite song when he was drunk on his whisky.

I remember when he used to tell me about his day.
Then tell me to change the channel to the football,
That's when he would fall asleep.

I remember when he used to cut our hedge,
Then fix the fence he had just put up.
Then he used to make a wheelbarrow to put into the garden,
Because it was too empty.

I remember when I left the house,
He used to wave me off from the window
And when all the grandchildren used to play with his hair,
He used to say, 'Give over!'

I remember when we were on holiday
And he used to wear white socks with his brown sandals.

And I know what it feels like to lose somebody
And I know that once they're gone, they're gone.
And I also know that time is special
And you should make the most of what you have of it,
Because you haven't got a second chance to make things better.

Sarah Blanthorn (12)
Hartford High School

MY FRIENDS

Claire is always looking out for me,
She's a good friend as anyone can be.
Then there's Nicola, solving problems is her thing,
But at a party, she tends not to sing.
Tui can be helpful, never a pain,
But sometimes she can be very insane.
Stephanie, she's the quiet one in the gang,
But in an argument she starts with a bang.
Joanne, she's the toughest of my friends,
If someone attacks us she's the one to defend.
Stacy's the one who's good at the talking,
She's like a robot who's always walking.
Those are my friends for all to see,
Out of all my friends, guess who's the lucky one, it's
   Me!

Nicola Hill (12)
Hartford High School

FAMILY AND FRIENDS

My best friend is really round the bend.
My mum's name is Jane and she'd like to go to Spain.
My dad's name is Andy and he's really handy -
He gives me lots of candy.
My brother is called Leigh and he hurt his knee.
My other brother is called Jordan and he is very small,
He also likes to play football.
My cat's name is Tia and her mum was called Mia.
My name is Anya and I like lasagne.

Anya Cobley (11)
Hartford High School

THE CARIBBEAN

The white sandy beach and palm trees
The glistening sun and the refreshing breeze
The cool clear blue water and exotic fish
The perfect place that's the perfect wish.
The monkeys conspicuous in the treetops
The amazing wildlife that never stops
The cool, clean seaside hotel pools
The natives huts, built using the most simplistic tools
The picturesque place where I would love to stay
The Caribbean, well it's not *that* far away!
Just thinking of that Barbadian beach
And the Bahamas, it's good they are easy to reach.
But what interests me the most is St Lucia,
Its scenic paradise, bright and colourful, like a fuschia.
I will travel to the Caribbean some day,
It looks so nice, I could be there to stay.

Andy Oakes (14)
Hartford High School

THE MONSTER

It swung its colossal talons like a farmer harvesting corn.
It flexed its other set of rending claws dangerously, enticing the enemy.
It bellowed as loud as a thousand foghorns, terrifying the opposition,
making it cower behind vegetation.
Its face grimaced menacingly like a clown at a circus.
Its shell glistened emerald like a precious jewel.
It emerged far above the canopy like a grand oak.

Alex Sylt (12)
Hartford High School

MY FIRST FOOTBALL MATCH!

The day itself was sunny
With people covered in green
The match is about to start
The first one I'd seen.

It's nearly started
The first whistle sounds
A cheer rises,
As the players enter the ground.

Kick-off, it's started,
The players run to position.
The ref and the ball have parted,
The match has begun.

'Foul, you're off!'
'He dived!'
'Get lost.'
A fight has just started.

'Goal!'
'Offside!'
'Shut up you fool!'
It's 1-0.

No it's full-time
Over already,
People spray wine
What a victory!

Craig Griffiths (12)
Hartford High School

The Magic Temple

Chorus
The freezing marble on the floor
The creaking noises from the door
The creepy pictures on the wall
The never-ending looming hall.
You will surely have a fright
Do not go to the temple at night.

Massive statues reaching the ceiling,
The cold, rushing wind in your hair.
The horrible chill in tonight's air,
Have you ever had that feeling?

Chorus

The eyes of the statues
All ruby-red.
Surely they're a warning,
You could soon be dead.

Chorus

Into the prayer room,
You better beware
They are listening and watching
The spirits are there.

Chorus

A magic carpet
Some blood on your sleeve
The spirits are rising
It's now time to leave.

Fraser Lindsay (12)
Hartford High School

119

I SHOULD LIKE TO RISE AND GO

I should like to rise and go,
To some place that nobody knows,
Maybe not too far away,
So I could come back in a day.
I should like to rise and go,
To some place that nobody knows,
Some place no one else could see,
Cocooned in my own sanctuary
I should like to rise and go,
To some place that nobody knows,
Somewhere near the swelling tide,
Where I could find a cave and hide.
I should like to rise and go,
To some place that nobody knows,
Maybe not too far away,
So I could come home in a day.

Sian Davies (14)
Hartford High School

PENGUIN

The penguin sat at the edge of the snow,
And dived in the water to catch some fish.
It came back up in two seconds flat,
With a mouthful of fish inside its mouth.

Most of its catch it gave to its child,
They must have been hungry and thirsty.
As they ate they cleaned each other,
And kept each other warm from cold.

Stuart Neyton (12)
Hartford High School

I Should Like To Rise And Go

I should like to rise and go,
Yon mountains high amidst the snow,
Where the wind's breath shears
From crevice to craggy peak.

Where the eagle soars,
Through scattered cloud,
Through ice and wind and hail,
Where the morning rays from behind the horizon,
Burst forth pure and clear.

To cliffs on high where slopes of grey and white,
Cascade in perpetual stillness
Here I feel at home,
Upon mountains high amidst the snow.

Samuel Walters (14)
Hartford High School

Mum

Short dark hair in a bob,
Her favourite horse is a cob.
Wide brown eyes so big and dark,
She used to take me down the park.
Always said she was in her twenties,
Chocolate ginger is her plenties.

Can be mean, but mostly nice,
Always afraid of little mice.
Her worst habit is snoring,
But she's rubbish at scoring.
That's my mum, she is the best,
And always wears a woolly vest!

Nicola Lander (12)
Hartford High School

THE MAGIC LAKE

Wolves howl at it by night,
Trees whisper its secrets,
And as it glistens in the moonlight
It seems to come alive.

I once walked down to this eerie place,
To seek its wonders and secrets.
But instead I found a lonely woman,
Sitting at its bank.

Wolves howl at it by night,
Trees whisper its secrets,
And as it glistens in the moonlight
It seems to come alive.

Her gown was as black as death,
And her eyes were pools of blood.
The lady of the lake she is,
Whom has haunted there for years.

Wolves howl at it by night,
Trees whisper its secrets,
And as it glistens in the moonlight,
It seems to come alive.

A twig crunched beneath my feet,
She turned her head and floated towards me,
Her eyes became daggers
And her hair became snakes.

Wolves howl at it by night
Trees whisper its secrets
And as it glistens in the moonlight
It seems to come alive.

I have never been to the river since,
In case I see those eyes again.
The lady of the lake they call her,
She perished in its waters.

Joanne Mycock (12)
Hartford High School

I SHOULD LIKE TO RISE AND GO

I should like to rise and go,
To the sun-drenched Costa Blanca,
Walk beaches of white, and see blue sea,
With no one there but me.

I should like to rise and go,
To the African Sahara,
Get chauffeur driven past lion and all,
And see them standing tall.

I should like to rise and go
To the ancient land of Egypt.
Stand and gaze at the great pyramids of old,
And see the sphinx tall and bold.

I should like to rise and go,
To the harmonious Easter Island,
Gaze upon the wonder of towering heads,
And rest in comfortable beds.

I should like to rise and go,
To the world where all is peace,
Enter the gates of the other side
And feel great peace inside.

Scott Heath (14)
Hartford High School

I SHOULD LIKE TO RISE AND GO . . .

I should like to rise and go,
Up tall mountains in the snow.

To sail down rivers near and far,
I don't care how long they are!

Flying high above the ground,
That's where I'd like to be found.

To walk the jungle, dark and creepy,
Or visit Egypt, sly and sneaky.

Wandering across the Atlantic Ocean,
To hidden lands, well that's my notion.

And most of all I'd like to do,
Anything I put my mind to.

Fraser McColm (14)
Hartford High School

A FAMILY MEMBER

If she was an item of furniture she would be a comfy chair,
                                        soft and cuddly
She is a doll because she is cool and trendy
If she was a drink she would be a glass of champagne,
                                        bubbly but stylish
If she was a colour she would be green.
She is pure silk because she is so gentle.
If she was an animal she would be a wolf because it's
                        agile and quick, but also mysterious.
She would be England because she likes to stay at home.

Sarah Dale (13)
Hartford High School

MY FAMILY AND FRIENDS

I've got a cousin called Holly
She's got a pretty dolly
I think her name's Polly
She gives Polly lollies.

My best friend's Emma
She has got a collection of feathers
She had a very big dinner
That's my best friend Emma.

My dog Sally is a fluffy thing
I wish she could sing
She gets on the sofa with my mum
But I think they are both dumb.

My dad snores really loud
I think my dad's head is up in the clouds
He has loads of pounds
He makes loads of noisy sounds
That's my dad - loud.

Laura Jones (11)
Hartford High School

IRAN

I should like to rise and go
    To where different fruits grow
Where the sky is clear blue
    Is where I love the most
To the place my eye first saw
    Where I touched the ball first.
        Iran.

Keivan Latifi (14)
Hartford High School

I Should Like To Rise And Go

I should like to rise and go,
Where mountain tops lay beneath the snow,
Where the sun gleams down on a layer of white,
And reflects in my eyes, all dazzling bright.

Through a misty, jungle route,
Hidden creatures howl and hoot,
To a cracked and dusty ancient tomb,
Inside of which dark shadows loom.

I'd trek across the desert dry,
Climb the pyramids and touch the sky,
These wonders I'd love to go and see,
But be sure to be back in time for tea!

Beth Jones *(14)*
Hartford High School

I Should Like To Rise And Go

I should like to rise and go,
To a mountain peak, where gales blow,
To a sandy beach with a scorching sun,
To Disneyland Paris, oh what fun!

To a small village with rolling hills,
To a luxury hotel with expensive bills,
To a country cottage where wild flowers grow,
To Venice to see the gondolas go.

On a camping trip to watch a starry sky,
And to hear the beautiful wild birds cry,
Then back home on a magnificent cruise,
Of all the places to be, home I would choose.

Sarah Hodgkinson *(14)*
Hartford High School

AM I A POET?

I've been asked to write a poem,
But I don't know what about.
I don't know how to write one,
Or how to set it out.

What topic should I use?
Should I make it funny?
Do you think it will get published?
Will I get some money?

I need some inspiration,
Where do I get it from?
Wait! I have an idea,
Oh no, I forgot . . . it's gone.

I've been asked to write a poem,
But I don't know what about.
I don't know how to write one,
Or how to set it out.

Carla Peters (15)
Hartford High School

SPACE

S   pace is out of this world
P   lanets in line waiting to be joined by space
A   liens walking around looking for something new
C   rafts waiting to lift up and up into space
E   arth sets in the west to sleep
    but space has only just begun.

Laura Smith (13)
Hartford High School

TRAVEL

I should like to rise and go
And travel overseas
To venture in the rainforests
Observing all the trees.

I would like to see the Earth
As a dot from outer space
To explore the world beyond the clouds
And look down upon this place.

I wish to view the pyramids
That tower above us all
I want to sit on the highest ledge,
And look down a waterfall.

Neil Jacob (14)
Hartford High School

MY IDEAS

My big, smelly fat cat sits on the mat
like a dead rat.

My stupid sister eats all day long,
like a pig gone wrong.

My mental dad drinks loads of Bud,
when he goes down the pub.

My furry dog looks like a hog,
when he comes back from the bog.

I like to sit in the sun,
but I get a burnt bum!

Katie Shepherd (11)
Hartford High School

3-0 VICTORY

My favourite sport is football
Man Utd are the best
The crowds roar
When Scholes scores
Puts United 2-0 up
Forty minutes gone, just another five minutes left, another shot
But the keeper saves it.

Second half
The crowd's more excited than before
A shot from Giggs
The keeper dives
The crowd jump off their seats
And roar for the third time
As the ball hits the back of the net.

Josh Thomson (12)
Hartford High School

I SHOULD LIKE TO RISE AND GO . . .

I should like to rise and go,
To a place that I've forgotten.
A place where I can swim all day
And dive to the sea's bottom.
Where there is not one cloud in the sky
And a place where all troubles escape your mind.
To this place I shall return,
One day before I die.

Jessica Scott (14)
Hartford High School

GAZZA

If he was a piece of furniture, he would be a rocking chair,
always on the move.
If he was a toy he would be a tennis racquet, people of all ages
liking him.
If he was a vegetable, he would be a pepper, not much inside
his head.
If he was a colour, he would be red as it is his favourite colour.
If he was a musical instrument, he would be a trumpet, loud and clear.
If he was a country, he would be the USA, always needed
for something.
If he was an item of clothing, he would be a pair of socks,
always smelly.
If he was an animal, he would be a dog, always wanting attention.

Ben Stott (13)
Hartford High School

THE FURNITURE GAME: MY BROTHER SEAN

As a piece of furniture he would be a Nintendo Gamecube
nearly always on and always active.
If he was a toy he would be a skateboard, always on the go.
If he was a fruit he would be a strawberry, always loved
and never lonely.
As a colour he would be blue as he is my favourite person.
If he was a musical instrument he would be a guitar, cool and brilliant.
As a piece of clothing he would be a T-shirt, never left out in an outfit.
If he was an animal he would be a reptile, no particular reptile,
he would not care as these little reptiles are his legs, all knobbly.

Liam Edwards (13)
Hartford High School

MY PETS

I've got a cat called Merlin,
I think he came from Berlin,
He's got really fat,
He's as big as a top hat,
He likes to eat mice,
He thinks they're very nice.

I've got a dog called Spud,
He likes to play in mud,
Once we took him for a walk,
He really wanted to talk,
Before he jumped into a puddle,
And got in a muddle.

I had a hamster called Harry,
He was very easy to carry,
Because he was so small,
He wasn't even as big as a wall.

I had a fish called Goldie,
It wanted to be a goalie,
It liked to play football,
It wasn't very tall.

Callum Bayliss (11)
Hartford High School

CORNWALL

I always go surfing when I go to Cornwall,
I love the Cornish ice cream.
I love the mall,
But I'm not allowed to buy anything because everyone is so mean.

Megan Cain (11)
Hartford High School

MUMMY

If she was some furniture she'd be a floor lamp, tall and bright.
If she was a toy she'd be a teddy bear, cute and cuddly.
If she was a fruit she'd be a grape, sweet yet picky.
If she was a colour she'd be blue, open and on top.
If she was an instrument she'd be a drum, loud and in your face.
If she was a country she'd be Japan, kind and giving.
If she was a piece of clothing she'd be a jumper, warm and soft.
If she was an animal she'd be a dog, fun and loving.

Lucy Widdowson (13)
Hartford High School

FIREWORKS

Boom goes the fireworks as you stand there
Fixed to one spot fascinated.
The exciting bang makes you jump inside.
The smell of burnt gunpowder makes my nose twitch.
The dangerous whistle of the rocket zooming over your head.
Spinning faster and faster the Catherine wheel goes.

Luke Hagan (13)
Hartford High School

ME

Me, what does that word mean? Who is me?
More importantly who am I?
I have no friends and no money.
What have I done to deserve this much pain?
I have but one question . . .
     Why me?

David Stevens (13)
Hartford High School

THE SIMPSONS

Homer Simpson is very fat,
The Simpsons have got a black cat.
Bart is really cool,
Likes to play in the swimming pool.
The program is on every day of the week
If you don't watch it, you're a geek!

Marge Simpson's got long blue hair,
But no one really seems to care.
Maggie Simpson sucks her dummy,
She always falls onto her tummy.
Lisa Simpson goes to the library,
At school she likes chemistry.

David Jones (11)
Hartford High School

TRAVEL

I would like to rise and go,
To where the sun will always glow,
Where mountains stretch far high above,
Beyond the reach of wren or dove,
There will be no one except me,
I'll be there and I'll be free,
New Zealand's where I'll rise and go,
It's where the sun will always glow.

Catriona Gilmour (14)
Hartford High School

FRIENDS

Friends are there when no one else is,
Friends can be anyone but especially kids.
Friends may make promises that they forget,
Or cancel a date that was set.
But friends will be there when you're in need,
And are always ready to do a good deed.
Some friends make you do the strangest things,
Some make you glad, as if you're flying without wings.
But one thing is always said about friends,
That they are always there for you whatever the outcome at the end.

Jessica Houghton (12)
Hartford High School

ANTARCTIC

The Antarctic is as cold as a freezer, only stronger
The weather is sometimes warm and sunny, but never hot enough
                                    to keep the animals warm
It is like walking into a room of white and blue
It looks like sky but with big, white clouds
It is a field or blanket that is covering an ocean of blue
Stalagmites hang in the deep depths of this sky-looking place
It is the odd one out that never sees the real heat of the sunshine.

Kelly-Marie Tuff (14)
Hartford High School

MY SNAKE

Eddie is fast and funny,
And fat in his tummy.
He's beautiful and clever,
I'll like him forever.
He's cute and smooth,
Apart from his groove.
He's my snake Eddie.

Sean Edwards (11)
Hartford High School

WHAT IS LOVE?

What is love?
Is it butterflies in my stomach?
Every time you walk by,
Is it stuttering every word?
As you stop to say hi.
Is it my legs turning to jelly?
As you walk towards me.
Is it holding my breath?
Every time the phone rings.
Is it my heart pounding frantically?
When you pass by my door.
Is it my body melting?
When you hold me in your arms.
Is it being trusting?
When you smile at my best mate.
Or is it the pain in my heart?
As you tell me goodbye.

Claire Owen (15)
Penketh High School

Broken Wings

My cage has crumbled,
and I am set free.

Because he is gone.

My wings unfurl,
and I soar through the air,
with just a gentle flutter.

Because he is gone.

My heart is filled with passion,
warmed with colours,
and the warm wind,
plays with my hair.
All day.

Because he is gone.

And the familiar evil sound,
begins to ring,
I try to hide.
Desperately try to hide.
But it is too late.

Because he is here.

My padlock is sealed.
I am trapped.
He watches me,
like a gifted eagle watches on his prey.
A cloud of black smoke fills my head.
His cold footsteps whisper,
he is coming closer.

His stuffy, stinging, stabbing hot breath
cools my face.
His malevolent eyes look into mine.
My black cloud has exploded.

Jessica White (13)
St Chad's RC High School, Runcorn

ALL ALONE

A cool dark evening, twisted into morning,
The cemetery is gloomy, family of lost ones mourning.

A name engraved on a single headstone,
Thinking of it now, all them people grieving must feel so alone.

She sits there, waterfalls falling from her face,
Her long brown hair mirroring her grace.

All alone.

At night she sits with a blanket, keeping her being warm,
She talks to the wind, telling it off for being so cold,
Though it has no shape or form.

She loved her husband,
Now that he has died, she'll never leave his side.

Days and months passed by,
In the same spot she sits, until months later she sadly dies.

All alone.

All this is coming from a tree,
Who sat alone and watched the old lady
All this is coming from a tree.

All alone.

Lisa Rimmer (14)
St Chad's RC High School, Runcorn

VOLCANO

A black river of anger,
Bubbles through my rocks,
My anger is like fire,
Hot! Hot! Hot!

I try to hold it back,
But I just can't help.
I finally reveal it,
My lava now to melt.

Emotions race through me,
Happy, sad, excited.
I spread all over cities
Although I'm uninvited.

Chopping down trees,
Buildings, shops, houses.
Banging, shouting.
Listen!
Noises! Noises! Noises!

I flow down each hill,
And work my way around.
Through cosy little cottages
Through cities to larger towns.

I then begin to cool,
With a trail or path to follow.
They all know where I've been.

What ever will happen tomorrow?

Jeni Reese (13)
St Chad's RC High School, Runcorn

SOULMATES

Look at me,
I have been cast aside.
A wave of emotion.
Washes over me like a tide.
I'm supposed to be a symbol of everlasting love,
But I have failed.
The love my owners had for each other,
Has de-railed.
A lover's tiff
Broke them apart.
It destroyed what they had
From the very start.
The special bond between them
Now broken.
Since last week
They have not spoken.
Engaged to be married next May
She caught him out at dawn
After trying to make things work
The love they had got torn.
The *slam* of a car door,
And two familiar feet,
My owner's back, the wedding is on
And now they're tied together with every heartbeat.

Two years later,
Another one has come.
They are strong together, a weight of three,
My work now is done.

Steffany White (14)
St Chad's RC High School, Runcorn

FOOTIE FEVER!

I've got my lucky shirt on.
I haven't brushed my hair,
I've even bought my programme from
That lucky seller there.

I haven't worn my *red* scarf,
Not since we lost 5 - 0, away.
But I really like this *red* shirt . . .
I hope we win today!

As I arrived at Anfield,
I was feeling excited,
But until,
A man standing next to me,
Was shouting for United?

My favourite player is Steven Gerrard,
No one can tackle him,
I know this because every time he plays,
We always seem to win.

The whistle blows,
End of the match come so quickly,
I've ate so many hot dogs,
They were very sickly.

Chelscie Jones (13)
St Chad's RC High School, Runcorn

CANTEEN

Tip-tap, tip-tap is the sound of the first person
Walking to their food.
Tip-tap, tip-tap, there's the second.
Rumble, rumble, the children

T
U
M
B
L
E

To their food.

They sit in big parties,
Eating, drinking, also thinking.
Talking, socialising, messing about,
All these children do is *shout! Shout! Shout!*

I can almost taste the sweet smell of chocolate pies,
The children are standing in big, long lines.

Briiiiiiiiiiiiiiiing!
That's the bell,
It was as *loud* as hell.

A minute ago

Now it's silent.

Nicola Roberts (13)
St Chad's RC High School, Runcorn

A BULLET OF LOVE

He was the boy next door,
Charming, sweet and funny
And she was the new girl,
Her face as sweet as honey.

They were made for each other,
Best friends in the neighbourhood,
Loved each other's company
One another they understood.

But the good feelings would not last for long,
For good things never do,
Her parents dragged her away from him
As he told her, 'I love you.'

She mourned the loss of her companion,
Lover, friend, soul mate
But friends and family did not listen
For him they truly hate.

She saw him and to him she ran,
Her love she no longer could hide
But her mother was ahead of her,
For the trigger did she find.

His body lay cold on the ground,
The girl screamed she could love no other,
She picked the gun up from the ground,
Killed herself - and her mother.

Rebecca Sargeant (13)
St Chad's RC High School, Runcorn

THE MONSTER WITHIN

Running through the darkness,
Glancing side to side,
Nervous system: *overload*
Tingles down her spine.

Have you ever had the feeling,
Of someone watching, following you?
This girl had that feeling,
Walking alone at half past two.

Footsteps growing quicker,
Break into a run.
Earlier she'd been with her mates,
But this was certainly not fun.

Suddenly that hand shot out,
Grabbing, roughly stealing,
And then he left her on the floor,
Alone with that dirty feeling.

Inside he left a monster,
Ever growing stronger,
Therefore she cared less and less
As it stayed there ever longer.

Now sadly here the story ends
Here comes a crazy twist!
To bleed the feeling from her skin,
She harshly slashed her wrists.

Courtney Reynolds (13)
St Chad's RC High School, Runcorn

NOT SPOKEN TO

I'm so far a   w   a   y
In the distant sky,
No one speaks a word,
To me,
Why?
    Why?
        Why?

Each day I *rise* for you
I'm your protective mother.
I give you warmth,
Light,
But you rebel with your words,
Why?
    Why?
        Why?

Seal up your soul with my tears,
Stop blaming me,
For all your fears.

Strands of clouds sail by,
I'm still sat there,
Burning alive in the sky.

When I go,
Darkness lingers,
I try to rest,
My sorrows away,
But where I lie,
Is where I die.

Until the morning mist arrives,
I come back alive,
To fight for life,
All day,
All night but,
Why?
    Why?
        Why?

Katie Page (13)
St Chad's RC High School, Runcorn

PIRATE BIRD

A tall misty killing machine stands alone,
No one passes its ghoulish zone.
The only sound that can be heard
Are the wimpish moans of Pirate Bird.
Thunderstorms roll all around
As a foolish man is drawn in by the sound.

Entering the death trap at a slow pace,
The door slam makes his heart race.
Hearing the door slam shut
Expression on Bird's face went bitter,
He swooped around thrashing through anything in his way.

Bird did nothing, man didn't leave,
Frustration turned to anger, Bird began to tease.
Reaching out grabbing an axe
Stalking the stranger ready to attack.
Slowly following into a black room
Bird made guest meet his doom.
A sudden sickening scream was heard,
That was the work of Pirate Bird.

Alexandra Parkinson (13)
St Chad's RC High School, Runcorn

SMOTHERED LOVE

The passionate, fiery love boils and steams
As the married couple stroll along the stream
His heart thumps and thumps as his love grew
She turned away as there was something she knew
He asked and asked her, she refused to tell
She stood up strong but weakly fell
As brave as a soldier, as weak as a fly
Her spectacular love was speeding by.

As from her cough came blood so red
So they sailed home and placed her in bed
The doctor was called in quite a hurry
The family gathered and continued to worry
The news was frightening; negative they could see
The doctor reported she had serious TB.

His pain grew and grew each hurtful day
He'd stand in silence and watch her pray
Her porcelain face, her golden hair
He'd speak no words, just stare and stare
Of a night he'd cry to sleep
Of a day he'd twitch and weep.

Then he snapped, insanity took place
He went and kissed her sleeping face
Reached for a cushion, held it down tight
Closed his eyes to block the sight
But as she gagged he began to cry
As he felt his world slowly die.

Natalie Sarsfield (13)
St Chad's RC High School, Runcorn

A BROKEN HOME

It was Will's fourth school of the year and he had lost all hope,
He wasn't eager to move again especially to Stanhope!

His mood as grim as a rainy day and his face as white as snow,
It's no wonder he likes to drift away to a place no one else can go.

'Cheer up' says his mother although she knows this can't be done,
She is aware of her drinking problem and how it affects her son.

'First impressions are everything,' she says, as she fastens his second
hand coat,
But Will knows this won't matter to the children of Stanhope!

Will doesn't get on with other children.
To them he's not quite right,
They tease him because of his looks and the fact he is not that bright.

His thin fragile body tries hard to fight the strong wind,
His mind on his father and all the arguing.

Although he has a mother, inside he is alone,
The only way of contacting his drugged-up father is by telephone.

He longs for a loving family and a house he can call his own,
But he knows this will never happen as he comes from a broken home.

He slowly rubs his aching arm from the bruises off his mum,
He's had many broken bones before like his nose, wrist and thumb.

He approached the end of the road and paused there for a while,
Then the overdose kicked in leaving him on the floor in a pile.

Will chose to end his life here as he had nothing worth living for,
He'd leave this world behind him for a better life than before.

Erin Smith (13)
St Chad's RC High School, Runcorn

The Eyes Of A Shop

A lot of different people
Pass through the doors each day
Fat, thin, long hair, short
I see the way they sway.

Some are upset or angry
A troubled mind I can tell
I see everything, they can't hide
The bitterness can swell.

But I guess you get some happy ones
Who bounce ten feet off the ground
With joy of how good their life is
They hum a sweet tune or sound.

They buy a lot of different things
From birthday cards to crisps.
It's surprising how many people are forty
And the stuff they buy as gifts.

Each aisle is filled with shopping
And the people just can't remember
Whether they needed to get chocolate
Or ice cream for December.

I guess as a security camera
I see all that happens here
From shoplifters to screaming children
If I were gone, it would be severe!

The people are my family
I recognise everyone of them
The things they buy are unusual
A bottle, a brush or even a gem.

Hayley Meagher (13)
St Chad's RC High School, Runcorn

SEPTEMBER THE 11TH

I'm sitting at my work's window,
Watching the day go by,
But something struck my eye,
It was a plane,
A plane coming towards my work,
I thought it was just my imagination,
So I rubbed my eyes,
I looked again,
It's even closer than before,
I start to panic, sweat,
I shout and scream,
But no one listened,
I tell them what's happening, I started to run down the stairs,
Puffing and panting,
No one cares,
That there's a plane coming our way,
I get to the last twenty stairs,
I hear a big roar like a lion,
It's coming from upstairs,
I start to feel heat and I hear screams,
I start to run faster,
Trying not to think,
I get out of the building,
All I can see and smell is fire,
I start to think,
If only they had listened,
They would have seen all the pain and the remembrance
Of September the 11th.

Laura Cliffe (13)
St Chad's RC High School, Runcorn

CEMETERY

It's a cold, wet afternoon in the cemetery nearby.

The wind is whooshing loudly, as the flowers come out of their paper,
and go into the sky.

The people who drive past haven't a care in the world.
Of the people who have a coffin filled of only bones and a lonely soul.

People's families visit more than they can count.
For their loved ones of whom they can't stop thinking about.

Water is dripping from their faces;
It's nearly making a puddle of water by their side.

The families are too upset to talk about the death of a loved one.

So they turn around, say goodbye, and once again start to cry.

Laura Dixon (13)
St Chad's RC High School, Runcorn

DEAD BUT AWAKE

I lie there and wonder,
What it would be like to get up and look yonder.

All I can see are the walls of this velvety box,
I would be delighted if I could just stand up and see my family.

I hear people gratifying, I have more of a life,
That is I, with neglect and strife.

Down the sides the slugs will slither,
The texture and smell makes me shiver.

It wasn't long ago that I died,
So I know all that lies outside.
Gravestones lie everywhere,
And a wall follows round to hide them there.

People drop flowers while they mourn,
Children going to school walk and yawn.

As I tell this story to thee,
The mud through the cracks slip in on me.
I feel nothing, I see nothing,
Yet I can tell this story.

Like a statue I lay still.

Emma Cattrall (14)
St Chad's RC High School, Runcorn

ROCK PARK

Early autumn's morning,
Leaves falling everywhere,
Silently rustling,
Hot, warm colours,
Red, orange, brown
Carpeting the hard black floor around the bare trees
Waving their skinny brown arms.
Afternoon is here
Children everywhere
Hiding amongst the leaves
Crunching
Squeals of laughter
Comments in the air
and barking
Break the morning's silence.
Late at night
The park is as cold as ice
Girls wearing next to nothing
They'll soon be coughing
Teens, off their faces
Rude happenings
First on their list of priorities
Waking up tomorrow
With a sore head
and many regrets.

Collette Davies (13)
St Chad's RC High School, Runcorn

HIM . . .

How I wonder where you are
As you linger in my heart
Are you waiting there for me
Or have you gone?
Do I want to see?
On I'll go as my heart aches
For your touch
Your smile, attractive looks
Your hand in mine
Tingles my spine
And I wonder, where are you?

Naomi Clarke (14)
St Chad's RC High School, Runcorn

BLOODY ROSE

It was done
She dropped the rose and ran
Her fingers were numb
He got too close
He asked for it
And already she was being haunted by his ghost.

Those words echoed in her head
But they didn't mean a thing
It was what Jake said . . .
To two other women
So she got a knife . . .
They're all the same . . . men.

Hazel Clarke (13)
St Chad's RC High School, Runcorn

ALL ALONE

I sit in my window
and watch them go by.
Although they never seem to notice
the tear coming from my eye.

I'm still young but as time goes by,
I will get old.
Please someone love me,
please take me home because life is not healthy
for a dog on its own.
I feel like an ornament waiting to be cleaned,
but my master the shopkeeper is
oh so very mean.

I've been here two years shedding my tears,
I don't think that anyone wants me.
Am I ugly?
Am I weird?
Is it that my fur's not gold?

I feel as hungry as a pigeon,
and as skinny as a twig.
I watch my master sitting there eating like a pig.
A family of three comes into the shop, and
I watched my master drown to a flop.
They looked at me and gave some comments
and referred to the shopkeeper.
They gave him money and said many thanks,
and took me in my cage.

I am as happy as a child with candy,
my new owners are very handy.
I have my bed and bark for food,
and they very rarely get in a mood.
I love my new home, I'm not all alone . . . anymore.

Fern Smith (13)
St Chad's RC High School, Runcorn

HIDDEN

I wore my new eye shadow today:
It's purple and blue.
But it changes from blue to purple to green and yellow
when it's not new.

I don't just wear it on my eyes,
it's on my arms too,
and my back and my neck and my chin and my legs.
It sticks to me like glue.

Mummy has to put more on each day,
I don't really know why,
When she does, it hurts a lot,
but I'll never cry.

If she's upset, she'll put lipstick on me
Not in the right place.
She always puts it on the insides of my arms,
but mostly across my face.

This lipstick tastes different, it's warm too.
It's really runny.
I spill it on my clothes and the floor sometimes,
Mum thinks it funny.

I think I'm too young to have make-up;
I'd love to look like you.
I always have to try and hide it, cover it up
or I'll lose Mum too.

Alysa Thomas (16)
Sir John Deane's College

TIME INTO DUST

The man?
No one set.
We waited till dark.
Anticipation creeping
Took a knife from the kitchen.
It would taste some different meat tonight.
The door locked, should anyone try to enter?
This is to be the first time, if not the last.

We went outside, surprised by how ordinary things were,
Clouds, no moon, people shuffling home.
Rushing to get dinner on or finish work.
Not for someone.
In the park, I chose a bench,
Good view, no cameras.
Waited.
Young woman, blonde hair, rejected.
Same as the next person.
Taking my time, I could come again.
Eventually a man walked by.
Hurried, thinking me asleep, homeless.
I took my chance.

We both remember that night, not such a big step for us.
How the man staggered. We watched.
His blood seeped into the ground as time froze.
The knife glinting crimson.
No remorse as I wondered who his wife was - ring on his finger,
And if she would scream with grief in the morning.
Her children deprived of a father, or no great loss.

I washed my hands. Rid of the blood.
As I remember your face, impassive like mine.
I knew you wouldn't tell, you laughed.
Considering what I had done, petty crime.

Soon our relationship, a curious mix of complex emotions
No need to lie or twist
To do so would be pointless
So still we dance around each other.
Taking moves, studying weaknesses,
Though we're on the same footing.

And people will never follow us.

Lindsey Tilston (16)
Sir John Deane's College

TRUTH, THE RIVAL

A wilting bloom with petals so green
Cannot pose with thorns to puncture you.
Then why magnify it in your mind's eye
To a stalking tiger between the weeds?

Why does it cycle through your dreams
Like chewing on rusty razor blades?
When it is of no more harm
Than the rotten fruit of paranoia.

Why is it the sickly flower
A fractured cope, mistaken likeness
Chokes you up at the roots?
It cannot steal your precious stamen
Only bud up its discontented wonder.

Shake free from its tendrils
Of blind uncertain dependency
No longer be unwilling nourishment
Let it wither to bulb
A bitter vegetable of remorse.

Matt Normansell (18)
Sir John Deane's College

THE COURT OF QUEEN SERTRALINE

Red, white and blue,
The colours of the Union Jack
Or of flowers in a newborn spring,
Or schoolgirls' brand new uniforms
Or a new start.

Purple, yellow and green,
A painting by a child as they splash
Their colours fearlessly
Or the confusion
Of an old woman's dress pattern,
Or an exciting mix of bright ideas.

Black and white,
Chalk on a board as they learn
The difference between right and wrong,
Or the division of a nation
Or the division of a mind.

Grey,
Of funeral suits,
Of sadness.
A million shades of monotony,
Each perched on the nightmare edge
Of a fragmented hope.

Blank,
Of nothingness,
Of a chemical induced despair
That can't even be felt.

Holding still,
Head in your hands.
Slip on your surgical gloves
And pretend that you touch nothing
And that nothing touches you.

Ruth Newton (17)
Sir John Deane's College

ALONE TOGETHER

All you lost you seek to find.
The pain you thought you'd left behind
Is still as fresh. It never leaves.
The wound is dry, but still it bleeds.

The tears you thought would sink beneath
Are welling up. A sea of grief.
The mourning songs that your heart sings
Don't dull the pain. Inside it stings.

And yet you see the flower bloom
Amid the haze of summer's noon.
The show goes on. The cameras roll.
But still inside the empty hole.

The mask that slips reveals your cry,
Scrutinised by the prying eye.
The fair facade that is the lie
Conceals your quest to reason why.

The show goes on. The cameras roll.
You must conceal the empty hole.
They do it too. They have the fear,
Subdue the pain and dry the tear.
Alone together in the game.
Our constant strive to be . . .

. . . the same.

Bernadette Flexen (16)
Sir John Deane's College

THE GENTLE BREEZE

She was lying on the grass,
under the willow tree.
The sun was shining, it was pure bliss
and there drifted a gentle breeze.

She lay there,
her soul torn apart.
Angry, depressed.
With an empty heart.

Bruised, beaten,
she feels so lonely.
If she'd told someone
if only, if only.

She feels there is no one
left in the world.
To help her and to convince her,
that she is an ordinary girl.

She spots a rope,
way up high.
Then she begins
to climb, but doesn't know why.

She ties a noose
around her head.
She jumps, she falls
she stops, she's dead.

Her spirit drifts
with the gentle breeze
The moral of this,
don't bully. Please.

Alexandra Maling (11)
The Queen's School

TERRIBLE TWINS

Terrible twins
Never think alike
If one is good
The other is bad,
If one is happy,
The other is sad.

Terrible twins,
Never think alike
If one says, 'I'm not tired!'
The other yawns, 'Goodnight!'

Terrible Twins,
Never think alike
If one says, 'Up!'
The other says, 'Down!'
If one says, 'Straight!'
The other says, 'Round!'

'Terrible twins!'
Shout Mum and Dad,
'Terrible Twins!
You're driving us mad!'

Terrible twins
Now think alike,
If one is good,
The other is good.
Now they both do
Exactly as they should!

Elinor Mayes (11)
The Queen's School

YOU ARE AS YOUNG AS YOU THINK YOU ARE

When I was young I was told
That it doesn't matter if you are young or old
You are as old as you think you are.

Let's for example take Miss Hare
She sits at home on her chair
Complaining all day about the new
But no one cares what she thinks,
Because they like her sister Mrs Hinks.

At a ripe age of ninety-two
She plays football with Dr Who
Dr Who is a scientist you see
And at the age of fifty-three
He thinks he's as old as old can be.

But their hearts are made of pure gold
As they are constantly being told
By the Honourable Lady Dee
Who lives in her stately home at 103
And thinks she's as young as me!

But of course *you* are as old as you think you are.

Lily Huggins (11)
The Queen's School

A LOVELY LIFE

How grateful I am to have had such a nice life,
With a family who care,
And a husband who is always there.

As I sit in front of my cosy fire,
Reminiscent of days gone by,
My happy childhood and tormented war years,
The joy of seeing loved ones return,
and the sorrow of those that didn't.

I knit my grandaughter a woolly jumper,
I know she'll never wear,
But at least the thought is always there.

I have seen it all from rations,
To mini skirt fashions.
When I look back over my life,
I feel fulfilled and content,
No desires to be a career girl,
Happy to be a mother and housewife,
Computers, drugs, mobile phones to me
Those things are never meant.

Katherine Baker (11)
The Queen's School

ALONE

Sitting in an ageing chair
Festoons of colour from
Daytime TV.

Isolated in memories,
Growing older and wiser,
But no one to tell.

Hissing of the fire
As it dies down
But no one to help
Keep it alight.

She wishes
And she prays
Someone will
Find her . . . alone.

Lottie Williams (11)
The Queen's School

A SNAIL'S TALE

Trailing silver on the ground,
Making not the slightest sound.
Slowly sliding while residing,
From the magpie he is hiding.
Shell so hard but still so frail,
Danger lurks for every snail . . .

Zoë Lambrakis (11)
The Queen's School

LOST YOUTH

Last year we had a grandaughter
I was simply over the moon
Until I was told
I was getting old
and I'll be in a nursing home soon.

I started to feel uncomfortable
A home was not my cup of tea
So then I jumped up
and I put down my cup
and I tried to run but I hurt my knee.

I then went on a bike trail
with people about twenty
I tried to keep up
but it was just too tough
and I realised cycling wasn't for me.

Next there was parasending
Skiing, climbing and abseiling
But all to no avail
At them all I was to fail
So my wife suggested I take up singing.

In the end I realised I was just too old
Not one thing active I could do
Then I thought of my life
and said to my wife,
'Well at least I'm not as old as you.'

Charlotte Dalton (11)
The Queen's School

LIFE

She's had a good life
But winter,
It came so soon.
Spring's child sits
On her arthritic knee. Playing

With the buttons on her
Much loved cardigan.
Her old weathered face breaks
Into a smile, as those innocent eyes
Gaze into hers.

She allows herself the memory,
Of her own innocent, carefree days.
Dancing in meadows, filled with buttercups,
Alas, she's jolted back
To reality, when her stick falls

To the floor with a clatter, then,
'Here you are Grandma,'
Says Spring.

Hattie Kennedy (11)
The Queen's School

COUNTRYSIDE JUNGLE

Rain tumbles down,

Grass absorbs drizzly shower,
Trees stand proudly.

Wicked winds whine
Ear-splittingly,
Petite cottages cough.

Wind kicks
Withered leaves.

Trickling stream cruises by,
Pebbles stand motionless,
No noise is heard.

Hedgehogs scuttle past,
Thin blades of solitary grass.

All is captivating,
All is intricate,
All is picturesque,
All is endearing.

Tabatha Leggett (12)
The Queen's School

OLD AND LONELY

When we came to collect her,
She looked very frail and old,
She just sat there in her chair,
In the gloominess, in the cold.

She took a while to get ready,
As her legs were stiff and old,
She showed us where the boxes were,
So we did as we were told.

When we got into the car,
Friends waved her away,
She looked so sad to be leaving,
Shame it was a gloomy day.

She made no expression,
When she got to her room,
Just sat in the armchair,
And remained in her gloom.

We checked up on her every week,
To see how she had got on,
Until the day came,
When we found out that she'd gone.

Harriet Williams (11)
The Queen's School

GETTING OLD

Getting old may be good,
In years to come,
It may be fun
To be old.

The sweetness to have grandchildren
To see the smile
Of their drawing
Of a crocodile.

Wouldn't it be fun
To have a slice
Of the past
To warm up the loneliest of houses.

It's about getting wiser
It's about teaching kids and grandchildren
How to deal with problems
That they might have.

It's fun to live to the very end,
But some things have to change,
Like winning bingo,
And getting those awful colds.

Emma Roberts (11)
The Queen's School

THE WINDOW ON THE WALL

She knew a boy called Jacob,
He attended her school,
He was a bully with a gun,
Who thought of himself as cool.

One evening she thought she saw Jacob,
Standing outside the window on the wall,
He was looking directly at her,
Seeming not to move at all.

She'd always been scared of Jacob,
So behind the sofa she went to hide,
But when she sneaked a look at the window,
She got a petrifying surprise.

Jacob had got out his famous gun,
He had it aimed at her head,
She screamed, the window was going to smash,
But when he fired, she was dead.

Jacob was not outside the house,
Neither was he not there at all,
For he was standing behind her,
She had seen his reflection, in the window on the wall.

Cheryl Laverick (11)
The Queen's School

GRANNY VS GRANDMA

On my mother's side of the
Family there's Grandma.
She's married to a Chinaman,
So I'm an eighth Chinese.
She has learnt to cook these
Dishes for my grandad. From
Watercress soup with black eyed beans
To fish, chips and peas.

On my other side there's Granny.
She married a local man who
Is humble and kind, the same
As my other grandad the one
who's Chinese.
She has learnt to cook these
Dishes for Grandpa. From
Sausages and mash potato
To fish and chips and peas.

But despite all their differences,
They both turned up to my
Sports Day. *Bang!* 'Let the granny race begin!'

Naomi McMullen (11)
The Queen's School

A SPECIAL PERSON

Her soft pale skin is no longer tight,
but ridged.
Her hair has lost its colour,
It's no more, blonde and glistening,
but silvery highlights lie amongst her hair.

She can't get about as easily any more,
and isn't as mobile.
She is absent-minded and is not as energetic as she used to be.

She gives me treats, and tells me tales of her past.
She's very kind at heart and cares lots about me.
She always squeezes me tight when she's worried.
But she'll always be my perfect granny!

Lucy Cope (11)
The Queen's School

A WIND POEM

Swords of rain lash down before me
Lightning as fierce as troops in battle,
Come forward, attacking our village.
The wind laughs as he tears roofs apart from terrified buildings.

Dragging me along in his powerful arms,
We head towards the foaming sea.
My spine tingles as the waters swallow me into the depth of his soul.

The waters embracing arms clasp me,
But then . . .
His anger is calming, his grip is weakening,
The wind stops, he's dying, he is no more.

Hannah Webb (11)
The Queen's School

FEELINGS OF OLD AGE

Absent-minded and awkward
Bewildered and bemused,
Careful and conscious,
Doubtful and dying,
Exhausted and elsewhere,
Frightened and frail,
Grey and grumpy,
Helpful and honest,
Interested and insecure,
Jobless and jovial,
Kind and knowledgeable,
Loving and lonely,
Magical, memories,
Nostalgic, neighbourly,
Old age is all these things to me.

Sophie Clough (11)
The Queen's School

LOVE!

Love is the greatest a wonderful thing
A symbol of love, a ring!
Love is about people having a spark in their life
Like a man proposing to his future wife
Love is having hugs and kisses
To cheer up the Mr and Mrs
Love is the greatest
A wonderful thing.

Lottie Daly (11)
The Queen's School

SLEEPLESS NIGHTS

Inside of my head
Are all of these thoughts
Made of yeses and nos
Made of crosses and noughts.

They are brilliant, inspired
Creative, thought-through
They are poignant and moral
They are vibrant and true

And so there sits my pen
Between finger and thumb
But as it's put to paper
My ideas all go numb

Where is my brilliance?
My yeses and nos?
Where is my vision
Of beautiful prose?

My pen sits on paper
My mind switches off
Was that just a dream
All those crosses and noughts?

So I flick off my light
I lie back in my bed
But again the words buzz
Rushing round in my head

And it's then that I'm clever
When the world cannot know
I have insight and life
But they've nowhere to go

So I sleep and I dream
And at morning I sit
With a pen in my hand
And a mind full of grit.

Kelly Siegel (15)
The Queen's School

MY GRANDAD

My grandad has millions of
wrinkles more than I can count.

My grandad has a mouthful of false teeth,
that limits him to what he can eat.

My grandad is going deaf,
he is so forgetful he can't be left.

My grandad falls asleep in front of the television,
while I am doing my revision.

My grandad loves his gardening,
but I think it's sickening.

My grandad is very sweet,
after Sunday lunch he takes me for a treat.

So this just about sums up my grandad,
but he is not quite so bad.

Cassandra Boffey (12)
The Queen's School

SEPARATED

There was nothing but the wind
blowing in his face.
He remembered the herd,
and picked up the pace.

He ran down the hill,
thinking of his mother.
With not a minute to kill
he ran up another.

He could see the herd in the distance
he remembered when his heart tore,
and from his loving family,
he was separated no more.

Rebecca Spaven (10)
The Queen's School

MARKET

There it was in front of me
A cruelly victimised horse in such a bad way to be
Its coat was white, but had shades of black
I was about to take it into the market to where it had belonged back
When someone confronted me
Demanding 10p
For the horse no one wanted, for the horse *I* was due to buy
Well, for the horse's sake I gave it a try.

So when I took it home, I decided to let it out for a run
And I started laughing to see the little horse having so much fun
It makes such a difference to see the horse walking with glee
From when it was tied up by the market, tied up to the tree.

Anneka Burek (12)
The Queen's School

AN OLD MAN

The old man that looked eighty
But was actually really seventy
His wife had died and he was upset and lonely
And his home is no longer homely.

He has a son of forty
And his son has a wife who is thirty
They have a child of ten
Who has a pet hen.

The old man was close to dying
And his child was very trying
The old man has written his Will
But has not paid one bill.

His child will have to fight
Until he has to write
When the good man died this morning
And that was the end of his snoring.

Zoë Hoult (11)
The Queen's School

LET GO

My life, my hopes, my dreams
All came crashing down.
I could no longer stay and smile,
No longer stop and dream,
No longer sleep at night,
No longer hold on tight.
So I let go of all I held,
And went, without a sound.

Fiona Meredith (13)
The Queen's School

My Magic Boxes

(Based on 'Magic Box' by Kit Wright)

Into my Jubilee box I will put . . .
the cheer from the crowd
when the Queen arrived,
the grand finale,
and the musical concerts.

Out of my animal's box I shall bring . . .
the proud roar of a lion,
the shake of the earth
when an elephant goes by,
and the noisy song of a blackbird.

Into my season's box I shall place . . .
the first bleat of a newborn lamb in spring,
the sweet scent of a summer flower blooming,
the first leaf turning orangey-yellow in autumn,
and the last snowflake in winter.

Out of my holidays box I will take . . .
the everlasting freshness
of the sea on a cruise,
the varieties of multicoloured fish
in the Maldives,
and the powerful surf in Cornwall.

The hinges on my box are a crocodile
opening and closing his vicious mouth,
the corners tell secrets
of the present, past and future.

The sides of my box . . .
are purple and velvet
and the lid is curved
like the setting of the sun.

I will hide my box . . .
at the top of a mountain
or in the depths of the sea,
waiting for the next generation to come.

Nicola Canfield (12)
The Queen's School

THE GIRL WITH GOLDEN HAIR

She sits there, in the classroom.
The silence shattered by midnight's chime.
She is not here, she is not there,
A lost memory from time.

Her eyes, red rimmed from crying,
Her vacant blue gaze stays dull,
Her skin white and pallid,
And clinging to her skull.

Her time has passed and been forgotten,
But she is always there,
A glimpse, a glance, a glimmer,
The girl with golden hair.

Kate Bernie (12)
The Queen's School

FREE!

One day, I will be free,
Free to roam
And to just be me.
Ruled by no one
Except for myself
Full of glory with mountains of wealth.
Free, free, free as the bee,
I want to love and
Be friendly.

I've been trapped
In this life too long,
I need to wander
And sing my own song.

Free, free, free as the bee,
I want to love and
Be friendly.

Laughing and playing,
Singing and dancing,
Running and jumping,
Oh to be free!

Free, free, free as the bee,
I want to love and
Be friendly

Today I am free.
Free to roam
And just be me.
Ruled by no one
Except for myself,
Full of glory with mountains of wealth!
Free, free, free as the bee,
I can love and
Be friendly!

Jenny Overton (11)
The Queen's School

SADNESS

Sadness is the feeling when someone close to you dies,
Your heart feels heavy,
You feel on the verge of crying every minute of the day,
And you feel as frail as a leaf, inside.

Sadness is the feeling when your friend moves away.
You think about them every day.
You wish to just see her face again.
But you know that will never happen.

Sadness is when you are being bullied.
You dread going to school.
Yet you will get grounded if you don't.
Tears form in your eyes at every word she says.

Sadness is a feeling, nobody can control.

Jennifer Hardy (12)
The Queen's School

THE MOMENT BEFORE THE BELL RANG

It was on a bitterly cold winter's day,
The grey clouds emerged from the dark, frosty sky,
There was a hurling wind that was fiercely blowing
                    gritty stones across the tarmac.
Whilst a silver, shiny, metal gate stood frozen and calm,
As the soft, silky moon appeared through the rustling tree branches.

The jet-black shadows perched upon the old shattered dusty windows,
Behind the dark quivering trees the old chimneys let out
                    pouts of smoke.
Then the old rustic bell rang with a loud hollow echo,
                    signalling the start of next lesson.

Laura Hogg (12)
The Queen's School

What Can You Do With A Balloon?

Hold onto the string
and fly up into space,
or you can sit on it
and bounce in a race.

A big hot-air balloon
for someone very small,
or a round sphere
to score in football.

A home for aliens
whose home is way up there,
you can cut it in half
so there's more of it to share.

Oh-oh, I shouldn't have done that
there goes a massive *boom!*
What can I do with
bits of balloon?

Elena McLoughlin (12)
The Queen's School